Stand On
Your Own Feet

"Natalie Smith has imbibed the peaceful dedication of the cloister and made it available to everyone—prisoner, shut-in, laborer. This book offers to those involved in business of any kind a key to opening their lives to God's grace in the midst of their daily responsibilities."

—Brother Gerlac O'Loughlin
Vocation Director, Abbey of Gethsemani

"*Stand On Your Own Feet* offers treasures of practical wisdom and spiritual experience."

—Father Charles Cummings, O.C.S.O.
Editor, *Cistercian Studies Quarterly*

"Natalie Smith clearly details the practical and necessary spiritual path of 'Anonymous Monks.' Her 'rule of life' embraces the ordinary austerities of everyone's life and helps transform them. . . . This edifying work will contribute to the building of 'Christ's Body' in ordinary but sacred Christian daily life."

—Jonathan Montaldo, Editor,
Dialogues with Silence:
Thomas Merton's Prayers & Drawings

Stand On Your Own Feet

Finding a Contemplative Spirit
in Everyday Life

Natalie Smith

ThomasMore®
— An RCL Company —
Allen, Texas

NIHIL OBSTAT:
Rev. Msgr. Glenn D. Gardner, J.C.D.
Censor Librorum

IMPRIMATUR:
† Most Rev. Charles V. Grahmann
Bishop of Dallas

December 14, 2001

The Nihil Obstat and Imprimatur are official declarations that the material reviewed is free of doctrinal or moral error. No implication is contained therein that those granting the Nihil Obstat and Imprimatur agree with the contents, opinions, or statements expressed.

Send all inquiries to:
Thomas More® Publishing
An RCL Company
200 East Bethany Drive
Allen, Texas 75002-3804

Telephone: 800-264-0368 / 972-390-6300
Fax: 800-688-8356 / 972-390-6560

Visit us at: **www.thomasmore.com**
Customer Service E-mail: **cservice@rcl-enterprises.com**

Printed in the United States of America

Library of Congress Contol Number 2001 134095

7480   ISBN 0-88347-480-8

1 2 3 4 5   06 05 04 03 02

Acknowledgments

The author would like to gratefully acknowledge the following persons for their great kindness and generosity in assisting both directly and indirectly in the development of *Stand On Your Own Feet*.

Brother David Steindl-Rast, O.S.B. www.gratefulness.org

Father Charles Cummings, O.C.S.O., Brother Patrick Hart, O.C.S.O., Brother Gerlac O'Loughlin, O.C.S.O., Abbot Basil Pennington, O.C.S.O.

Jonathan Montaldo (Thomas Merton Center at Bellarmine, Louisville, KY)

Audrey Santo (Advocate for the Comatose, and mother)

Sammy Diaz (Prison Ministries)

A Carthusian Monk at the Charterhouse of the Transfiguration

Brother Michael Batton, O.C.S.O., Abbot Flavian Burns, O.C.S.O., Father Anthony Delisi, O.C.S.O., Abbot Bernard Johnson, O.C.S.O., Sister Lillian Shank, O.C.S.O.

Lay Cistercians Liz Allison, Linda Boland, Santino DeJohn, Crunch Fox, Louise-Marie Moise, Sharon Newman, Terry Nicholson, Liz Romano, Doris Saulle, Mary Ann Wunker, Angela Zephrin, and Mark Zittle

Father Francis Akwue and Father Martin C. Devereaux

Joseph Bonnaig, Ann Brefka, Wilma Davis, Linda Hammerle, Mike Johnson, Nahyla Mateus, Jessica Nigra, Carol Orlove, Jacqueline-Therese Rychlicki, Ronald Serra, Mary Jane Serra, Michael Siebert, Chad Smith, Christian Smith, David Smith, Faith Smith, Jeremy Smith

Debra Hampton, John Sprague, and associates at Thomas More Publishing

Contents

Foreword

The city of San Francisco honors one of its citizens with a most unusual memorial. We have all heard of memorial hospitals and memorial libraries, but how about a memorial turnaround? The Friedel Klussmann Memorial Turnaround is part of San Francisco's cable car system. It consists of a few yards of tracks, mounted on something like a giant lazy Susan embedded in the pavement of Ghirardelli Square. When it turns, it reverses the direction of the cable car standing on it from downhill to uphill. Then the car can be hitched to the cable that will pull it up the steep incline of Hide Street to the top of Nob Hill.

As I was standing in a long line of tourists waiting to board the cable car, the idea of a "memorial turnaround" kept tickling my mind. Suddenly the thought hit me: Couldn't one call the whole Christian tradition the "Jesus Christ Memorial Turnaround"? Doesn't it go back to a turning point in his life when he broke bread with his friends and said, "Do this in remembrance of me"? Wasn't his short life a turning point in history? Didn't he turn people's minds around by the way he lived and taught? "The last shall be first, and the first last." "Let the greatest among you become as the least, and the ruler as one who serves." This is nothing less than the blueprint for a monumental turnaround in both public and private life, a call for total conversion.

"Conversion" is a word that has lost much of its bite. Today, even Christians have almost forgotten that it literally means a complete "turnaround." The early followers of Christ, however, were well aware that their way of life ran counter to accepted standards. "When I am weak, then I am strong," Saint Paul said. But when the early fervor cooled off, and Christianity gained worldly power, a crying need for another turnaround arose. This time, it was the turn of monks to be out of step with an aging society for the sake of Christ's Good News.

Saint Benedict, who gave monastic life in the West its lasting shape, called the monk's turnaround not *conversio* (conversion), but *conversatio*, which is the Latin word for an *ever repeated* conversion. A monk was to be mindful of the example of Christ and apply the call to conversion to every detail of daily living. This became the driving force for monasticism as a counterculture able to challenge and reshape society.

Today, we need another turnaround, "to use things and love people, not love things and use people." We need another transformation of society; our very survival depends on it. More and more Christians of different denominations are turning to Saint Benedict as a teacher and guide as they tackle this task. Many of them are not monastics but "Anonymous Monks," as Natalie Smith calls them—"people of all ages and of all religious, economic, and social backgrounds who desire to live a prayerful life living and working in the modern world." Many of them are formally connected with a monastery of their choice as members of the extended monastic family. They often outnumber those living in that monastery, ten, twenty, or thirty to one, and their numbers are steadily growing—a striking phenomenon of our time, and one of the more encouraging ones. It is for these Anonymous Monks that Natalie Smith wrote *Stand On Your Own Feet*.

This is a nuts-and-bolts book. Natalie Smith applies the turnaround principle to a wide range of tasks confronting busy people in their private and professional lives. The book deals with shopping, reading, eating; with television, child-rearing, fashion, peer pressure, money, sex, sickness, and many similar challenges. The Table of Contents will give you an overview.

You will notice how often prayer is mentioned in the chapter headings. For Natalie Smith, praying means more than saying prayers. She sees prayer as a power that changes the world—the source of kinetic energy for the turnaround. In prayer we go to that core of our being where each of us can say, "I live; yet not I, but Christ lives in me." When we act from this center, everything we do becomes prayer—prayer-in-action that changes the world.

Stand On Your Own Feet is a book about basics, yet it is not for beginners only. Time and again, all of us need to go back to the basics and make a new beginning. As we practice the prayer that changes the world, we ourselves will be changed. We will discover that our conversion implies more than we realized on the basic level. We may discern social implications that go far beyond what we bargained for: "We are on a protest of sorts" (Merton).

Natalie Smith does not draw out all the implications of the turnaround. She follows accustomed patterns of Christian thought and expresses herself in accustomed language. Once you learn to stand on your own feet, however, you will sooner or later hear a call to go beyond everything to which you are accustomed. Precisely because you are grounded in tradition, you will be able to renew tradition, seeing it in a new light and expressing it in new language and initiative.

My own path has shown me this. Half a century ago, my life as a young Benedictine was close in its outward form to the life of a medieval monk. Today, I am serving Anonymous Monks in more than a hundred countries through an interactive website, www.gratefulness.org. More and more far-reaching changes are undoubtedly awaiting us. All who learn from this book to stand on their own feet can sing with conviction the famous Shaker refrain, "To turn and turn shall be our delight, till by turning and turning we come 'round right."

Brother David Steindl-Rast, O.S.B.
www.gratefulness.org

Prologue

Listen carefully to the master's instructions,
and attend to them with the ear of your heart.

RULE OF ST. BENEDICT, PROLOGUE: 1.

Through this book I am passing on a way of prayerful living that stands on its own under any circumstances, a way for busy people to live holy lives no matter their personal circumstances or professions. I am speaking of eternal, unshakable freedom, the freedom to truly be and know ourselves. My intention in writing this book is to help discover who we really are by helping to rid ourselves of what we are not. Finally, I believe that we can experience union within ourselves, union with others, with God, and with all creation. What peace, harmony, security, and happiness!

Thomas Merton was a famous Trappist monk, activist, and inspirational writer, who rarely left his monastery, Gethsemani Abbey in Trappist, Kentucky. After twenty-seven years of cloistered life, Merton, inspired by God, took a journey to Bangkok in 1968 to deliver a message on the subject "Marxism and Monastic Perspectives." Within hours after having delivered his message, he was accidentally electrocuted.

Contained in Merton's last address are several key statements that are vitally important if you are going to understand the helpful spiritual reflections contained in this book. In what turned out to be his final address in Bangkok, Thomas Merton, a.k.a. Father Louis, made the following remarks midway through his discourse:

I spoke to another Tibetan lama, a young one whom I consider a good friend of mine—a very interesting person indeed. Chogyam Trungpa Rimpoche is now about thirty-one or thirty-two years old. . . . He had to escape from Tibet to save his life, like most other abbots.

When he was faced with the decision of leaving his monastery, he did not quite know what to do. He was absent from his monastery on a visitation to some other monastery, and he was caught out in the mountains somewhere and was living in a peasant's house, wondering what to do next. He sent a message to a nearby abbot friend of his, saying: "What do we do?"

The abbot sent back a strange message, which I think is significant: "From now on, brother, everyone stands on his own feet." To my mind that is an extremely important monastic statement. If you forget everything else that has been said, I would suggest that you remember this for the future. From now on everybody stands on his own feet. This, I think, is what Buddhism is about, what Christianity is about, what monasticism is about, if you understand it in terms of grace.

Our living in a peace-filled family, workplace, school, society, and world largely depends on each individual person.[1] Ultimately, every one of us must take responsibility for maintaining an attitude of love amidst the ordinary events of daily life.

Outlined in this book are helpful suggestions, a way of living, whereby we can stand on our own feet, take responsibility for our own holiness, and discover who we really are. Using this book as a guide, we can stand on our own feet under the harshest circumstances, such as illness, legal problems, loss of job, bad relationships, imprisonment, and (like the Dalai Lama) oppression.

Many of the ancient rules and the lives of the saints have been encouraging. Often, however, they do not specifically address the situations experienced by those who are not living in a monastery or convent. We are teachers, nurses, students, professionals, housewives, patients, and prisoners who may be unaware that there are millions of others like ourselves seeking the same deep relationship with God through prayer.

A rule is a guidebook for living that instructs a person how to live his or her life in such a way that everything he or she says or does becomes prayer. Real prayer. Not just a passing thought of God now and then. Everything becomes prayer because in everything there is something that is done or not done for the love of God. In the clothes we wear, in the food we eat, there is some element of God that we are bringing into each activity of our lives. This is what a rule helps a person to accomplish.

Like a rule, the following series of reflections has been created in order to prayerfully unite, support, and comfort ordinary people who want to live a life dedicated to prayer amidst their particular circumstances. Through living out the principles contained in this book, we will learn how our lives can make a huge difference to the entire world. Together, we will channel our energy by focusing on the love of God and the needs of others. At the same time, God will receive the energy of our prayer and generously return it to the whole human race in the form of grace. This grace will enable others and ourselves to be healed and restored into the image and likeness of God. It is very exciting to know that from our homes, offices, hospital rooms, or cells, we can save the world.

This is not the type of book that one reads only once, sets aside, and never picks up again. This book is meant to be our companion throughout life. Each chapter was written to be meditated on and pondered. Each day, with the help of God's grace, we can read a part, examine ourselves, and reflect on the ways that we can develop and perfect our call to holy living. The spirituality outlined here is one by which, through the humility of an austere lifestyle, we will draw nearer to God. It will not only lead us closer to Jesus, but like John the Baptist, our lifestyle will have the power to point the way of salvation to the entire human race.

I present this series of reflections in the spirit of John the Baptist, for the blessed Baptist himself equated the humility of austerity with growth toward God when he said, "He [Christ] must increase, I must decrease" (John 3:30). Because John decreased, because he humbled himself, God greatly exalted him and drew others to God. We can be sure that our effort to live an austere life will have the same effect on the human race, right where we are. We can be sure that, if we adapt some of these precepts into our lives, many others will be drawn to Christ, to healing, to love, and ultimately to eternal life.

To give a more concrete example, I once read a story about Laura Bridgman. She was a young girl during the mid-eighteenth century who, because of a childhood illness, could not talk, see, or hear, and had poor sense of taste and smell. Her only sensation was touch. She was a predecessor of the great blind-deaf mystic Helen Keller. After reading about Laura's condition I thought about how thrilling it must have been for Jesus to heal the deaf and the blind. We probably cannot imagine the jubilation of a blind person suddenly seeing. We cannot imagine how unbelievably shocking it must have been for a deaf person suddenly to hear their first sound. How new and exciting it must have been for them—every sound bringing with it the triumph of a choir of angels, each new sight announcing the joy of their own private resurrection from darkness and isolation to sharing in the communion of sight and sound with others.

I thought about how overjoyed I would be each day for the rest of my life if I could bring sight and hearing to just one deaf or blind person. How greatly I would rejoice with them in everything that they would see or hear thereafter. Two or three hours after thinking these thoughts, I read further about Laura Bridgman and discovered that Laura's world came alive one day when a man named Doctor Howe taught her a sign language that was supposedly invented by Trappist monks in Spain. The monks apparently used the manual finger alphabet in order to keep their commitment to silence (*Helen Keller: A Life*, p. 16). When Helen Keller was being taught the manual finger alphabet as a young girl, she was full of elation as she suddenly realized that everything had a name. She ran around her yard and house feeling objects as the teacher (Annie

Sullivan) spelled into Helen's palm as fast as she could. I thought to myself, there you have it! The monks are bringing sight to the blind and hearing to the deaf not only visibly with sign language but invisibly as well with prayer. I realized that this incident of the monks helping Laura Bridgman and Helen Keller was an outward sign of an interior reality that the Trappists, and all those who are devoted to prayer, are bringing sight to the blind and hearing to the deaf.

At Mass the next day, I felt renewed vigor, surety, and joy that I could share in every good thing gained by those who were now truly hearing with spiritual ears and seeing with spiritual eyes because of the effect of my prayers. For the rest of their lives and for all eternity I would have a share in the joy of their continual new life. For me this share means a deep communion and immersion with others and with the Holy Trinity that goes far beyond a communion of words. It is a communion of the life that dwells in us by the Holy Spirit.

Jesus gave sight to the blind and hearing to the deaf. He also promised us: "Whoever believes in me will do the works that I do, and will do greater ones than these, because I am going to the Father" (John 14:12). We do greater works than Christ because of the power of the Holy Spirit to reach the whole world at once through our participation in prayer. This is why Saint Therese of Lisieux is known as the patron saint of missions. Like John the Baptist, she heralded the whole world to Christ by the power of an austere and prayerful life. By our prayers and by our desire to live simply, we also participate in a global evangelization.

We may not be able to give up all our material possessions and enter a monastery. For some of us who are financially secure, our austerity may be only interior, an austerity that never manifests itself outwardly. (Besides, contrary to popular belief, having money can carry its own fair share of suffering, burdens, and responsibilities, which for some are valuable sacrifices.)

Ordinary persons who are called to this lifestyle of humility through practical austerities are referred to throughout this book as "Anonymous Monks." Anonymous Monks are people of all ages, religious, economic, and social backgrounds who desire to live a prayerful life living and working in the modern world. [2]

As in all vocations, some who are experiencing the beginnings of this calling may not even be aware they have it. This is where the term "Anonymous Monk" originated. It was coined by Karl Rahner, a German Jesuit priest and theologian who wrote about persons he called "anonymous Christians." These are persons of all faiths and beliefs who experience the Holy Spirit working in their lives without realizing it, above their human conscious awareness. [3] This is especially true of the oppressed, the chronically ill, and the imprisoned. God is at work in these seemingly dismal circumstances without our realizing it.

Conversely, we may lead a life of continual good deeds without the awareness that all true good comes from God alone. We may achieve great status and renown in the arts, sciences, politics, and finances, not realizing that God is the source of all of our advancements. Like a farmer planting the seed and nurturing it, ultimately we realize that it is God alone that makes our efforts grow.

We may find ourselves entering into situations in life that we wish we could avoid. We may feel that our circumstances are possibly the worst in life. We may feel as though our life is coming to an end. We may feel that things have become so severe that suicide is the only way out. Little do we realize that our circumstances have slowed us down enough so that we can now hear from God in a way that would not have been possible if we had continued on as we were. In reality, God has saved many of us from ourselves and for this we should be grateful.

Many of us do not realize how much we have in common with monks living in a monastery. Like monks, many of us are already living lives of seclusion, not just physical, but emotional, spiritual, and mental seclusion. As humble monks submit to the authority of the abbot, we all must learn to lovingly submit ourselves to the will of God. Like monks, many of us eat and dress simply. For the benefit of those who are imprisoned, like prisoners, monks also refer to their bedrooms as "cells."

Monks practice what is known as "asceticism," which means basically "living without luxury." For some of us, living without luxury could mean not using butter or not buying that extra pair of shoes that we really don't need. A monk is a person who willingly and joyfully lives a strict, simple, and secluded existence. The monk is called to these circumstances for the salvation of the world. So, why can't an ordinary person living under similar circumstances out in the world do likewise?

God helps us to see our circumstances as bringing salvation to the world. To see how valuable all of our austerities really are. Negative experiences can be viewed, not as the end of the road, but as only the beginning, the beginning of eternal life. A life where nothing exists outside of God, which is all love.

The monk and his austerities are a constant reminder to God that his Son, Jesus, shed his blood so that souls can go to heaven. So also is the Anonymous Monk. By our austerities we show our faith and belief that there is a life to come and that this faith is pleasing to God. We show our faith by willingly letting go of our attachments. We use things and love people, not love things and use people. Our life is a protest of sorts (Thomas Merton). We have chosen to embrace our circumstances as a point of contact that says we are willing to abide with the lowest of the low because we are certain that nothing exists forever but God. Even the wealth of good health, the wealth of coming and going as we please, and the wealth of doing whatever we wish, whenever we want—we are willing to let all of these things go. No one or no thing can harm us because we willingly and joyfully lay down our rights to anything. We are truly free.

Even if we own many possessions, as long as they don't own us, then we have discovered true freedom. It is not our actually giving everything up that counts; it is our willingness to do so at any time.

By the practice of these suggestions we hope to literally abide in love, the only thing that will last. If some of us have had to give up many things, we try not to feel sorry for ourselves. Let's not put the emphasis on what we are giving up but instead on what we are gaining, which is God himself. We are also gaining a higher level of conscious awareness by clearing our minds and lives from a lot of useless clutter. In other words, we are able to think more clearly and even perhaps experience a great increase in our intellectual capacity. Yes, I am saying that by living simply we will be more open to God's wisdom and we will have more clarity in our thinking. This means we have more brain energy to focus and to think. I have heard that Albert Einstein didn't even remember his own telephone number for this reason.

More importantly, the more we clear our minds of complicated thoughts, the more we will know the will of God for us, the more we will be able to hear the Holy Spirit as he speaks to us. So, besides becoming more spiritual, we are also edging closer each day to human as well as spiritual perfection. Each day, we are returning to what we were in the garden of Eden before the fall of man.

The word "monk" comes from the word "mono," which means "one" or to be "alone" with God. Eventually we will all find ourselves standing naked "alone" before God where we must willingly and joyfully let go of all possessions, resentments, and desires before we will enter eternal happiness. The only desire that will aid our entry into eternal bliss is the desire for God alone, "literally."

So, we can now see how valuable this gift of being an "Anonymous Monk" is, of being alone with God. We can now realize how valuable our confinement is, be it physical, mental, spiritual, or emotional. Now, we can joyfully endure more self-denial than we ever thought possible. We will realize how something as simple as picking up a piece of litter can have a great changing effect on the world (Saint Therese of Lisieux). When we use our energy to restore our environment, to live for others, this energy has a resounding effect and is saving the world.

We will realize that from our home, office, hospital bed, jail cell, or anywhere else, we endure all toward saving the world for the love of God. (I will also include in these reflections special helps for those who are oppressed, chronically ill, imprisoned, or who may feel that their current state in life is of little value. I will also speak to those who are "locked in" a comatose state.) We can all focus our energy by emptying ourselves for the salvation of all. If you know of someone who is too sick to read, please read this book to them daily. The sense of hearing is often the last thing to go. Even though a person may be "locked in," mentally ill, or seemingly incoherent, often he or she can still hear. I have been told by friends of the comatose that they are reading to their "locked in" loved one every day. These persons often seem stripped of human dignity. Like Jesus hanging on the cross, they appear dead but, nevertheless, they live. They carry within themselves a life force that is valuable to God.

There are basically three types of situations that would be an indication of the beginnings of a calling as an Anonymous Monk. [4]

1. A person receives a direct call from God, as with Moses and the burning bush (Exodus 3:2).

2. A person, wishing to follow the good example of monks and nuns living in a monastery, takes on the holy task of imitating them as in imitating the saints (*John Cassian: Conferences*, p. 83).

3. A person is initially forced to live a monastic life due to mental or physical illness, oppression, or imprisonment, such as Joseph in the Old Testament who was sold as a slave by his own brothers (Genesis 37:27).

Whether we are called, desire, or happen to live a monastic life is not important. All are valid. With the help of God's grace, this book will be a source of support and will provide practical ways of developing this lifestyle. In order to understand logically, and perhaps theologically, the workings of this vocation, Anonymous Monks should have knowledge of the term "pluralism" [5] as it is used by the Cistercian Order of the Strict Observance, an organization of contemplative Catholic monks also known as the "Trappists."

For our purposes, "pluralism" is understood as an appreciation of the fact that as Anonymous Monks we need to adapt the common customs of a monastic spirituality to suit better our own circumstances. Some common monastic practices, such as scheduled times of prayer, have been modified, not in order to "make life easier," but to live with "greater intensity and austerity." [6] Through pluralism, we plan our prayerful practices by doing what can be accomplished in a peaceful manner and without drawing undue attention to ourselves. This practice of performing prayerful practices, only to the degree in which they are barely noticed, is in imitation of the Blessed Mother herself who "treasured all these words and pondered them in her heart" (Luke 2:19).

Through pluralism, monasteries adjust the details of spiritual practices according to their own local circumstances. We, as Anonymous Monks, also make adjustments, not because of slothfulness or lack of desire, but because of circumstances that are beyond our control, circumstances in which God places us. In other words, we wholeheartedly wish to complete our prayerful practices as monks in the monastery do, but through "no fault of our own," we can't. [7] God, the perfect judge, sees the willingness of our hearts, and this is what matters.

Similarly, we see God's perfect judgment regarding the good thief who was crucified with Christ. God knows that the good thief would have lived a life of total dedication to Christ if he had lived. Instead, the good thief (without baptism) responded to his calling in paradise. For those who do not know, the good thief expressed belief in Christ as he was being executed (Luke 23:43). Because of the willingness of his heart, the good thief was justified. His calling was valid and was not taken from him because the circumstances, primarily his own execution, were beyond his control. (I add this reflection for the benefit of those who may be on death row, or for those who may have only recently found out that they are likely to die soon. I want you to realize that the length of time that you have been given the calling of Anonymous Monk is not important.)

In Sacred Scripture, Jesus speaks of workmen who came in the morning, afternoon, or evening but who all received the same pay (Matthew 20:1–16). It does not matter how long we are willing or able to fulfill this vocation in life or how many crimes we may have committed. Even if you have been a serial killer, do not despair or let anyone tell you that you are not eligible for heaven. The devil is busy telling each one of us every day that we have committed too many sins, that we are unforgivable. Do not believe it. The devil is jealous of us all because we are children of God and have dignity greater than any earthly president or king. The devil knows this. We are valuable. God will not remember our sins against us, if we are as sorry as we can be. Believe me, I am telling you the truth. A saint once said, "God's heaven will not be complete without you."

As with monks in the monastery, we hope to build our lives around praying the Psalms. [8] Anonymous Monks experience a more perfect form of prayer when praying the Psalms, because we pray, in unison, the inspired Word of God. In other words, praying the Psalms is better than our praying our own prayers off the top of our head, so to speak.

Monks in the monastery usually pray the Psalms at regular intervals seven times a day. We may not be able to adhere to the same strict schedule as these monks do. This is one of the places where pluralism comes in. We must sometimes adjust the times and the way in which we pray, in order to better fit our own individual circumstances. This is done to avoid the distraction of the "out of order-liness" that can take place when we try to force a monastic practice, such as praying the Psalms, at a time and in such a way that our prayer is hectic, and our minds are not recollected.

We must remember to pray in such a way as to remain at peace. This is how, as mentioned above, pluralism "intensifies" rather than "makes prayer easier." When we are at peace, our prayer is intensified, as opposed to being fragmented when we spout out a bunch of prayers in a hectic or meaningless fashion.

It is better to say only a short prayer with all of our attention than to say many lengthy prayers with little attentiveness and sincerity. As Anonymous Monks, our schedule for praying the Psalms can be more general. Anonymous Monks must work diligently in order to simplify our lives in anticipation of breaking for prayer. Like the monks in the monastery, when we are not praying the Psalms, we fill our prayerful day with a collage of other monastic practices, which include spiritual reading (particularly the Bible) and work.

Through the use of these reflections, we literally do everything with an element of reverence for God. So that all energy of thought, word, and deed has meaning and purpose for God. Like Joseph and Mary, desperately seeking Jesus in the Temple (Luke 2:41–49), we are constantly and actively seeking union with God every minute of every day. By always remaining in at least one of the monastic practices mentioned in this book, we seek to remain in a state of constant union with God. If we do this, we have been successful, we have done our work faithfully.

At each point of contact, this dance with God, rather than tiring us out, energizes us. Over time, we move from glory to glory, moment to moment (2 Corinthians 3:18).

As it is written in the constitution of the Cistercian Order of the Strict Observance, Anonymous Monks believe that "fidelity to the monastic way of life . . . is our way of participating in the mission of Christ." Therefore, Anonymous Monks are faithful to their calling if they build their life around the liturgy, praying the Psalms, and are continually found faithfully resting in one of the other monastic modes mentioned.

Outside of praying the Psalms, we will know which monastic mode is right and "grace-ful" because it is the one that brings peace and order to our lives. [9] We become more loving to those around us. Through gradually developing the monastic modes developed in this book, we become alone with God in the confines of our hearts. We learn to invite God into every area of our lives.

From the food we eat to the clothes we wear, we hope that everything we do has meaning and is pleasing to God. In the end, we will find that we have completely redefined our understanding of recreation. The word "recreation" comes from the word "recreate." We learn to "recreate" ourselves anew each time we pray the Psalms and are reminded of the truth about ourselves, the truth that we are made in the image and likeness of God and that God loved us so much that he gave his only Son that we might have life, life that will never end.

We will find that we spend most of our leisure time praying the Divine Office (Psalms), and reading Sacred Scripture and spiritual writings. A Trappist abbot once remarked: "One learns to find his enjoyment and rest in the liturgy" (Psalms). He also described Trappist monastic life as "relentless." To some, "relentless" could be the definition of the spirituality outlined here in this book. But this is okay because many of you have known much hardship, and this is the way God would have it. This way you are strong already and not easily destroyed.

This is the kind of courage that it takes to live by these reflections. Through implementing the various disciplines outlined here, the Anonymous Monk finds the balance, the ability to mesh two seemingly contrary lifestyles, a life of contemplation (alone with God) and a very active life in the world (crowded with people).

Finding the time to pray and live according to the suggestions outlined is a sign of a great purification (Origen) that could take a lifetime to develop. Through practicing the virtues of patience and fortitude, we hope to endure faithfully in order to rule and reign with Christ eternally. When practicing these suggestions it is very important to remember that we are only responsible to do what we are able —this is what counts. Some of us, because of sickness, cannot do everything outlined, but this book will help us and others to understand the value of our afflictions.

We should not be discouraged by the severity of the challenge to love as God loves, but rather encouraged that we have been considered worthy of such a high calling with John the Baptist as our role model. Remember how highly Christ spoke of John when he said: "Among those born of women, no one has arisen greater than John the Baptist" (Matthew 11:11). Through the spirit of John the Baptist, we hope to travel deeper into the wilderness, into the desert of our own hearts, where we willfully and joyfully respond to the voice of one crying out, the voice of John the Baptist: "Prepare the way of the Lord, make his paths straight" (Mark 1:3).

As Anonymous Monks, we join Saint Bernard along the Cistercian way when he says:

> Our way of life is an awareness of our need. It is humility, it is poverty freely accepted, obedience, and joy in the Holy Spirit. Our way of life means learning to be silent, exerting ourselves in fasts, vigils, and prayers. It means working with our hands, and above all clinging to that most excellent way which is love. It means furthermore to advance day by day in these things, and to persevere in them.
>
> I trust this is what you are busily doing. There is one thing you have done at which everyone marvels. It

is that, although your lives were holy, you thought nothing of this but made it your business to share the holy lives of others that yours might become yet more holy. It is so rare that anyone leading a good life is ready to do this, that when it happens everyone admires it.

The Cistercian family welcomes you with open arms, and the angels look down upon you with smiling faces. They know very well that what pleases God more than anything is brotherly concord and unity, since the prophet says: "Gracious is the sight and full of comfort, when brothers dwell together in unity" and again: "When brother helps brother, theirs is the strength of a fortress." [10]

1. *Merton: A Film Biography*, Dalai Lama.
2. *The Call to Holiness*.
3. Karl Rahner, *Encyclopedia of Catholicism*, p. 1078.
4. *John Cassian: Conferences*, 3, ch. 4.
5. Statutes on Unity and Pluralism, 1969.
6. *The Golden Epistle*, reference notes, p. 17.
7. *Catechism of the Catholic Church*, 1281.
8. Trappist Constitution, ch. 19.
9. *Sayings of the Desert Fathers*, p. 83.
10. *Love Without Measure*.

ꕥ Chapter 1 ꕥ

Your Prayer Changes Our World

Let us get up then, at long last, for the Scriptures
rouse us when they say: "It is high time for us
to rise from sleep" (Romans 13:11).

RULE OF ST. BENEDICT, PROLOGUE: 8.

ꕥ**W**hat I present here in chapter one has to do with "kinetic" energy, which is the force or energy that is created by motion. Specifically, for our purposes, I am referring to the energy that is created through our own decreasing, our emptying of self, through the practice of humility. This is my attempt at a scientific explanation of the vocation of John the Baptist—the energy that his humble austerities created and the saving effect that these energies continue to have in the lives of others.

There is a passage in Scripture referred to as the "kenotic" hymn (which derives from "kenosis," the doctrine that Jesus relinquished all divine attributes to experience human suffering—not to be confused with the scientific term "kinetic") that could have some relevance for us in terms of the energy created by humility:

> Let the same mind be in you that was in Christ Jesus, who, though he was in the form of God, did not regard equality with God as something to be exploited, but emptied himself, taking the form of a slave, being born in human likeness. And being found in human form, he humbled himself and became obedient to the point of

death—even death on a cross. Therefore God also highly exalted him and gave him the name that is above every name, so that at the name of Jesus every knee should bend, in heaven and on earth and under the earth, and every tongue should confess that Jesus Christ is Lord, to the glory of God the Father (Philippians 2:5–11).

As Jesus and John descended into the depths of humility, we also can ascend and participate in so great a calling as the redemption of humankind. The *Merriam-Webster Dictionary* defines asceticism as "self-denial for spiritual reasons." Realistically, as ordinary people living in the world, we can literally deny ourselves things, or we can own things without them owning us. As regular people, we may often have to choose between inward or outward acts of self-denial. Either way, what effect do these acts have?

In the following paragraphs, I will attempt to offer a rational, perhaps scientific, explanation regarding the effect of prayer and self-denial on our world today. One of the greatest scientists who ever lived was Sir Isaac Newton. Few know that this great mathematician and physicist also had an interest in mysticism and theology. Part of Newton's early experiences included the study of an area of natural philosophy that saw all nature as being united as one. [1] This reality of nature is now more commonly referred to as the ecosystem.[2] In the ecosystem all of the functions of each individual plant and animal have some effect, great or small, on all nature globally. In the same sense, the physics of the spiritual life, like the ecosystem, is also one, or better put, one body in Christ. In the body of Christ all are one, so that everything that takes place, whether great or small, good or bad, has some effect on the "whole human race." [3]

This delicate balance is all about energy and how it is used, to bless or to curse, by the choices that each individual makes. In this sense, ascetic practices can be scientifically and logically understood.

Fundamental aspects of asceticism have much in common with laws of physics such as "cause and effect" and in Newton's third law of motion, "for every action there is an equal and opposite reaction." [4]

With physics in mind, let us reflect on the greatest ascetic act that was ever performed, the crucifixion of Christ. "No one has greater love than this, to lay down one's life for one's friends" (John 15:13). The purest use of spiritual energy for Anonymous Monks is to descend into the abyss of humility through obedience unto the point of death.

For some of us, this could mean a very real interior death to self-will. This is the dynamism of the crucifixion of Christ, almighty God in glory coming to earth in the form of Jesus Christ, all the kinetic energy of God's glory conserved, condensed, in Christ: "Who, though he was in the form of God, did not regard equality with God as something to be exploited" (Philippians 2:6). Condensing this energy Christ "emptied himself, taking the form of a slave" then humbled himself still further by his death on the cross, for "unless a grain of wheat falls into the earth and dies, it remains just a single grain; but if it dies, it bears much fruit" (John 12:24).

Through the dynamics of asceticism, Christ reversed the curse handed down to Adam and Eve, the children of disobedience, living for themselves. He willfully "humbled himself, becoming obedient to death, even death on a cross." In view of the redemptive force of the crucifixion, Christ "came so that they may have life, and have it abundantly" (John 10:10).

Through humility, the ascetic, like Christ, also learns to receive insults and persecution [5] and "as Christ humbled himself, becoming obedient to death" the ascetic humbly offers that energy back to God as Christ did in the violence of the crucifixion, sincerely praying to the Father: "Father, forgive them; for they do not know what they are doing" (Luke 23:34).

This prayer that Jesus prayed as he hung on the cross is a counterpart to what monks and nuns throughout the centuries have referred to as the "Jesus prayer": "Lord Jesus, have mercy on me, a sinner." As with Christ on the cross, the Jesus prayer is the pivotal point of the transfer of energy. When an ascetic wishes to consciously transfer his energy to the Father, especially in times of temptation, he may take a deep breath and utter the Jesus prayer.

Instantaneously, as the ascetic breathes out, he can feel the immediate release and transfer of energy. This breathing out after the Jesus prayer is that same breathing out mentioned in Scripture: "Then Jesus, crying out with a loud voice, said, 'Father, into your hands I commend my spirit.' Having said this, he breathed his last" (Luke 23:46). Immediately after Jesus exhaled, the dynamics of the transfer of energy was so evident that those watching were saved and astounded. "When the centurion saw what had taken place, he praised God and said: 'Certainly this man was innocent' " (Luke 23:47).

One can only imagine the reactive dynamics of this energy being conserved and offered back to God at the crucifixion. With the transformation of this energy, one can only say that it must have held the power and force of countless nuclear explosions. Carrying enough force to save the "whole human race" forever. [6]

Through the dynamics of "cause and effect," the energy of the glory of God has been transformed into the divine energy of grace. [7] Like a nuclear explosion, this divine energy "came from heaven" with "a sound like the rush of a violent wind" by the Holy Spirit at Pentecost (Acts 2:2). Each ascetic willfully seeks to add more and more to this dynamism by offering to God all energy of thought, energy of word, and energy of deed, so that it, too, can be transformed and added to the divine energy of grace poured forth upon the earth "for the salvation of the whole human race."

B elow are a few examples of ascetic/monk practices in which an ascetic participates by grace and the use of the Jesus prayer, in a global evangelization:

1. Through humility, energy retention associated with the reception of personal honor and praise is let go and offered up to God and transformed into grace. [8]

2. Through chastity and celibacy, sexual energy is conserved and transformed. [9]

3. By rejecting temptations to waste energy through malice, slander, and unjust anger, energy is conserved and rerouted for the salvation of the world. [10]

4. By letting go of bitterness from the past, the mental energy of the memory [11] is unleashed and offered up to God.

5. By remaining in the enclosure, unless required to leave because of obedience or obligation, energy is retained and offered to the Father. [12]

6. Proper body postures such as standing, bowing, etc., assumed during the sacred liturgy are important sources of energy. Remember the story recounted in the Book of Exodus, during the battle between Israel and Amalek: "Whenever Moses held up his hand, Israel prevailed; and whenever he lowered his hand, Amalek prevailed" (Exodus 17:11).

7. In regard to the chant, let's recall the words of Saint Augustine who said: "He who sings, prays twice," the reason being, that it takes more energy to sing than to speak.

8. Through the practice of obedience, ascetics go beyond their own capacity in order to join forces with others. Through obedience to superiors and each other, cenobites and hermits concentrate their energy, causing an increase in the dynamics of spiritual force and velocity. It is important to understand that the degree to which each individual member conforms to the saying of the Lord: "For I have come down from heaven, not to do my own will, but the will of him who sent me" (John 6:38) is the degree of the force of each one's ascetic practices. The entire monastic community becomes what many monastic writers have referred to as a "nuclear plant," or a "powerhouse of prayer."

These practices, along with much of what is mentioned in Saint Benedict's rule for monasteries, are all about the rerouting of energy. An ascetic must be willing to unleash every energy so that by grace all is trans-formed in Christ, leaving nothing hoarded, repressed, or wasted for the sake of one's own self-pity, resentment, or glorification. As in the parable of the talents (Matthew 25:14–30), the ascetic makes good use of all his time and energy. Through the dynamics of asceticism ascetics fuel the energy of life-giving grace for the salvation of the "whole human race."

Even though historians seem to have failed to see a connection between Newton's own spiritual interest in mysticism and theology and his scientific work, nonetheless, the connection is there. Many may now come to see Sir Isaac Newton as one who was "truly seeking God" through his own vocation as a scientist. [13]

With all this in mind, let us reflect on the following quote from the Cistercian constitution:

> Fidelity to the monastic way of life is closely related to zeal for the kingdom of God and for the salvation of the whole human race. Monks bear this apostolic concern in their heart. It is the contemplative life itself that is their way of participating in the mission of Christ and his church and of being part of the local church.

1. Microsoft Encarta 98 Encyclopedia.
2. Microsoft Encarta 98 Encyclopedia.
3. Trappist Constitution, ch. 31.
4. Microsoft Encarta 98 Encyclopedia.
5. John Climacus, *Ladder of Divine Ascent*, p. 161.
6. Trappist Constitution, ch. 31.
7. *The Philokalia, The Complete Text*, p. 262.
8. Saint Benedict's Rule for Monasteries, ch. 7, Humility.
9. John Climacus, *Ladder of Divine Ascent*, Step 15, Chastity.
10. John Climacus, *Ladder of Divine Ascent*, Step 9, Malice.
11. "Ascent of Mount Carmel," Book 3, ch. 3:3.
12. *Collected Works of St. John of the Cross*, p. 728, #9.
13. *Rule of Saint Benedict*, ch. 72:11.

☙ Chapter 2 ☙

Everything We Do Is Prayer

What is more delightful than this voice
of the Lord calling us? See how the Lord
in his love shows us the way of life.
RULE OF ST. BENEDICT, PROLOGUE: 19.

Contemplation of God can be understood in more than one fashion. For God is not solely known by way of that astonished gaze at His ungraspable nature, something hidden thus far in the hope that comes with what has been promised us. He can also be sensed in the magnificence of His creation, in the spectacle of His Justice, and in the help He extends each day to the running of the world" (*John Cassian: Conferences*, ch. 1:15).

The truth of the matter is that there are aspects of prayer in everything at all times. In a broad sense, prayer or contemplation is the presence of Jesus at work in all matter for the glorification of God. The earth is full of the goodness in which we contemplate God. Even the air that we breathe is the presence of Jesus giving us life. Every breath is our clinging to God for life. The air that we breathe today is the same breath of God in Adam (Genesis 2:7) and the breath of Jesus on his disciples (John 20:22). If we just hold our breath long enough, we will be instantly reminded of our utter dependence on God. And this utter dependence is also referred to in contemplative circles as the gift of "clinging to God."

From the very beginning, all of creation has been locked in this perpetual contemplative dance with God—God, who is expressed in the midst of creation's variety, moving, dancing, stirring, waxing, waning, groaning. The challenge for us, as contemplatives, is to stay in step with this contemplative rhythm of creation by relishing Jesus (his glory, God's glory) in all things and in every person without disruption. In other words, when the Jesus dwelling in us is truly appreciating the Jesus in the world, this present moment of union is a kind of contemplation.

Psalm 148 bears witness to the reality of this contemplative dance between creation and its Creator:

> Praise the LORD!
> Praise the LORD from the heavens;
> praise him in the heights!
> Praise him, all his angels;
> praise him, all his host!
>
> Praise him, sun and moon;
> praise him, all you shining stars!
> Praise him, you highest heavens,
> and you waters above the heavens!
>
> Let them praise the name of the LORD,
> for he commanded and they were created.
> He established them forever and ever;
> he fixed their bounds, which cannot be passed.
>
> Praise the LORD from the earth,
> you sea monsters and all deeps,
> fire and hail, snow and frost,
> stormy wind fulfilling his command!
>
> Mountains and all hills,
> fruit trees and all cedars!
> Wild animals and all cattle,
> creeping things and flying birds!
>
> Kings of the earth and all peoples,
> princes and all rulers of the earth!

Young men and women alike,
old and young together!

Let them praise the name of the LORD,
for his name alone is exalted;
his glory is above earth and heaven.
He has raised up a horn for his people,
praise for all his faithful,
for the people of Israel who are close to him.
Praise the LORD!

In general, whenever anything existing in creation—the planets, birds, trees, grass, storms, fish—are acting in accordance with the Father, they are contemplating, fulfilling God's purpose.

Remember the very important roles played by the tree of life and the tree of the knowledge of good and evil (Genesis 2:9). And of course, let's remember the greatest tree of all, the tree that supported our Lord during his crucifixion. (I must add how much I admire trees for their stability. Whenever I sense the urge to move about and wander in body or soul, I note the courage and steadfastness of the forest and the trees who stand as sentinels erect before God without wavering.) Not only does creation contemplate as humans do, but creation will also be judged and held accountable as we will also be. Remember how Jesus even cursed the fig tree for its not doing its job (Mark 11:14).

So trees, birds, things, all have a very active contemplative ministry in creation. Likewise, if we as human beings are doing the will of God, we are in a sense contemplating. If a surgeon is engrossed in brain surgery by the will of God, he is contemplating. If a teacher is engrossed in the enlightenment of the minds of others, he is contemplating. If a mechanic is engrossed in an oil change by the will of God, he is contemplating. If we are reading something by the will of God, we are contemplating. If we work with our hands by the will of the Father as Jesus the carpenter, we are contemplating. If we pray by the will of God, we are contemplating. We dance the dance of contemplation when we stay in step with the will of the Father by the fulfillment of his plan.

R ules for contemplative orders of men and women, such as the *Rule of Saint Benedict*, present a plan of life whereby a person can consciously flow from contemplative mode to contemplative mode throughout their day. This series of reflections is meant to assist ordinary persons in doing the very same thing by helping them to understand that when we do our best to open ourselves to Jesus at work in us, we are contemplating.

In my attempts to explain contemplation, I will begin from the time that we have little or no cognitive or conscious awareness of this presence of Jesus at work in us, to the time when, God willing, we become more cognitively aware of Jesus contemplating in us.

As with the anonymous Christian and the baptism of desire, in the very beginning stages of contemplation we are not consciously aware that many of our actions and thoughts are originating from the presence of Jesus dwelling in us, operating through us. Whether we are aware of him or not, Jesus is still there. And because of his presence within us, contemplation is taking place to some degree.

People of all ages, including babies and children, experience contemplation. It could probably be said that children are experiencing a purer form of contemplation than the rest of us, because, for the most part, they are innocent and their minds have not yet been polluted. Remember how the psalmist said: "Out of the mouths of babes and infants you have founded a bulwark because of your foes, to silence the enemy and the avenger" (Psalm 8:2). This is also why Jesus said: "Let the little children come to me, and do not stop them; for it is to such as these that the kingdom of heaven belongs" (Matthew 19:14). No image is more suitable for contemplation than that of the face of a baby. If this were not so, Jesus would have come to us as something else other than an infant.

Persons who are chronically ill, be it physically or mentally, persons who are retarded or comatose, also possess an effective form of contemplation whether they have cognitive awareness of it or not. God knows they do the best that they can with the grace that God has given them. God has special graces for those in special situations. Because of the severe simplicity often imposed on the chronically ill, and their not muddying the waters with their own desires, Jesus is surely there in all of his intensity. Jesus living in them as a burning torch, a powerful source of intercession for the world. In all of their nakedness, the chronically ill, the oppressed, and imprisoned stand before God as a constant reminder of the poverty and helplessness of humankind for whom Christ sacrificed himself.

I once knew of an infant who was born in a comatose state and remained that way for many years. When the Lord was asking me to forgo some of my favorite food items, I often thought of the heroic virtue of this child who lay in a bed all her short life, never experiencing the joy of a cookie or a cup of hot chocolate. Every day, as the sun was obedient to shine, she lay steadfast, unwavering as a true sentinel watching over the city of God. In a very real sense, she was like the abandoned Christ—not many people even knew of her situation.

I felt drawn to make a visit and sit next to her on the bed in order to warm myself and draw strength from the blazing inferno of contemplation that was surely there within this innocent child. Unfortunately, before I could arrange a visit, she died. I felt as though God had been waiting for someone to relieve her before taking her home.

I felt in some small way that I had relieved her, that I was now holding the fort, even if it was only for our little part of the world. I had now voluntarily agreed to give up the comfort of many of the food items (sweets and caffeine) that she was forced to live without. I also made a stronger resolve to spend more time in prayer by staying in my cloister (my home) as often as I could as she was so strictly forced to do. She seemed to have been a source of extraordinary graces that gave me greater courage to live for "God alone."

This child reminded me of Abraham interceding for Sodom and Gomorrah, that Yahweh promised to spare the city if there were only fifty . . . forty-five . . . twenty . . . or, finally, ten innocent people in the city" (Genesis 18:23–32). I believe because of the presence of this one innocent youngster that God has had mercy on us and blessed us.

For those who grieve, I would like to add that grief has the great potential of stripping from us all that is not God, leaving us denuded, feeling hopeless, and helpless. Grief allows the presence of Jesus in us to be more fully exposed and creates in us an attitude of intense anticipation of the mercy of God. Our entire being clings to the presence of God in our sorrow.

On the journey back to God, we often fill our lives by mourning the passing death of our own ideas and desires, much as our Lord mourned in the garden at Gethsemani: "I am deeply grieved, even to death" (Mark 14:34). "Abba, Father, for you all things are possible; remove this cup from me; yet, not what I want, but what you want" (Mark 14:36). We not only grieve the death of ourselves but also the death of others as Jesus and the sisters of Lazarus grieved over the death of their brother (John 11:33).

Let us also remember the intense grieving of the Blessed Mother that took place at the crucifixion of her only son. If grieving and mourning were not such a great blessing and such a deep form of contemplation, we as followers of Christ, along with our Blessed Mother, would not experience so much of it. Remember that it is Jesus in us who mourns while at the same time his presence within us is our comfort: "Blessed are those who mourn, for they will be comforted" (Matthew 5:4).

In time, if we are graced and persevere, we may obtain a greater cognitive awareness that Christ is operating in us, in all people, and in all things and events. As we grow in this awareness, we will experience an even greater appreciation of the true value of Jesus living in every person. We will be mindful that in every situation, in every occupation, every religion, there is an element of virtue, an element of Jesus, an element of grace and contemplation taking place. I am including every profession no matter how ordinary, mundane, or perhaps even sinful.

Prostitutes, alcoholics, prisoners, murderers, and the like, are often aware that something is not right, something is not working, but they just can't seem to place their finger on what it is. We all suffer from ignorance, but we do not despair. Even in sin, there are some aspects of grace, some source of contemplation taking place to some degree. God, have mercy on our souls.

As time goes on, some persons reach a more fully expressed, conscious form of contemplation and feel called to this formal lifestyle of contemplative prayer as if called to an occupation, or a full-time job, like a monk in a monastery. This fuller state of contemplation in prayer can be defined as the highest level of conscious awareness that Christ, who is all love, is praying in us. With this cognitive awareness we fall silent (apophatic, imageless prayer), realizing that something sacred is taking place within us.

Contemplative prayer is the awareness of Christ's love beaming in us, while we let him pray. I am not talking of a person who says flippantly, "Oh yes, Christ is praying in me." I am talking about our sincerely decreasing through humility to the point that Christ has increased and can pray through us freely without our getting in the way. This is contemplative prayer in the fullest sense of the word, the Son of man shining through the soul that has vanished through the sincere practice of humility so that it has become transparent, allowing Christ's love to shine through. It is then "no longer I who live [and pray], but it is Christ who lives in me" (Galatians 2:20).

Those persons with conscious awareness have to work constantly at the practice of humility to remove the obstacles that block Jesus praying in us. Humility means that we prefer the will of God (speaking to us through others) over our own. Humility means that we are willing to let go of anything because we truly believe that we have all that we need in Christ. Humility is the sincere willingness to let all things go, a willingness that could withstand the test of letting everything go if necessary. (Often, this actual letting go is necessary in order to advance in contemplation, because even the slightest love of things can block the love of Jesus in us to some degree.)

In order to maintain this humility and contemplation, a person must continually unite himself or herself through obedience to the will of God. We must be on guard constantly, for the devil would like to break our contemplation by causing unnecessary petty division between ourselves and others. The devil likes to test us to see if we can be distracted from our contemplation. But do not hand over your gift at any cost. Instead, pray for those who persecute you. Do good to those who hate you. Bless and do not curse (Luke 6:28). This response takes humility, and it takes obedience.

I f we commit sins of pride when we sit down to pray, the thought of the sin will stand before us like a shield blocking Christ's prayer in us. This fact should tell us that it is a sin to insist on our own way, to close our hearts to anyone through disobedience and pride. We remember the warnings of Christ that if we even call our brother a fool in anger, we are liable to judgment (Matthew 5:22).

Because of our pride we give up contemplation, which is so powerful a form of intercession. Our contemplation is Christ standing before the Father praying in us.

If we are not willing to allow Christ to pray in us by humility and obedience, if we allow sin to shield his prayer in us, then those who would have been saved are now hurt or perhaps lost because of our negligence. "From everyone to whom much has been given, much will be required; and from the one to whom much has been entrusted, even more will be demanded" (Luke 12:48). If Jesus called the fig tree to give an account, how much more so will God ask us to give an account for this great gift of contemplative prayer.

So, as you see, this lack of humility, this lack of obedience, is a serious matter. We are shepherds of the flock. We safeguard the flock by our contemplative prayer. We will have to give an account if we allow bitterness or prejudice against anyone to crop up in our souls and hurt the faith of any of these little ones by blocking Jesus praying in us. Instead, we should constantly pray to the Father: "Father, forgive them; for they do not know what they are doing" (Luke 23:34).

This prayer of contemplation is the risen transfigured Christ unhindered by the flesh, shining radiantly before God in the presence of all the saints. A soul in the act of contemplative prayer is experiencing Jesus, our powerful high priest, who has broken through the veil of pride, avarice, lust, envy, anger, sloth, and gluttony and has entered into the holy of holies to bring God's life to the world. Jesus in us is the Lamb of God, who by his sacrifice has offered himself for the sins of the world. Jesus is praying to God through us. Jesus is standing before God because we have allowed him to go to God through us by our willingness to decrease through the practice of humility and obedience.

At the height of contemplation, we experience the presence of Jesus helping, playing, teaching, doctoring, fishing, cleaning, hugging, suffering, through us. Note that the peak times of contemplation mentioned in the New Testament amount to what Catholics call the joyful, sorrowful, and glorious mysteries.

What could be more contemplative than an angel speaking to us (the annunciation)? What could be more contemplative than our helping a friend in need, especially when we are in need ourselves (the visitation)? Ask any woman who has given birth, what could be more contemplative than the labor experienced where every fiber of our being, every cell of our body, is fixed in the present moment on the life-giving task at hand (the nativity)? Contemplating the suffering of Christ (the sorrowful mysteries) has the wonderful effect of causing us to cling to God. And contemplating Christ glorified reveals the glorious mysteries that, after our souls have been purified, yield their harvest, and cause all creation to shout in praise of God.

I must also warn that those of us who do not allow Christ to be expressed through us, to contemplate in us in this lifetime, run a formidable risk. Imagine a place where there is a complete absence of matter. Where there is a complete absence of anything good, a place of purification, a place that weans us off our disordered love for things after we have died, a place often referred to as purgatory. (As I have stressed throughout this chapter, we must seek to understand that there is goodness all around us: in a soft chair to sit on, in the wetness of our tears that graciously moisten our eyes, in warmth and in a breeze, in insults and in suffering, and in giving glory to God through our perseverance.)

In purgatory, we feel the charring effects of the void, a state where the fullness of happiness (beatitude) seems far away like a great light in the distance. Purgatory is a state where we are frozen in a pattern of waiting for our disordered love for matter (vice) to be irradiated in us so that Jesus (virtue) can dwell fully in us. (I can tell you that this process is much easier to manage in this life than in the next.) Better to allow Jesus to dwell in us now, to open ourselves to him through humility and obedience in this life, moving and changing from glory to glory by degrees, rather than have it happen all at once in the state called purgatory. What I have said throughout this chapter has all been said by Christ:

> "I am the true vine, and my Father is the vinegrower. He removes every branch in me that bears no fruit. Every branch that bears fruit he prunes to make it bear more fruit. You have already been cleansed by the word that I have spoken to you. Abide in me as I abide in you. Just as the branch cannot bear fruit by itself unless it abides in the vine, neither can you unless you abide in me. I am the vine, you are the branches. Those who abide in me and I in them bear much fruit, because apart from me you can do nothing. Whoever does not abide in me is thrown away like a branch and withers; such branches are gathered, thrown into the fire, and burned. If you abide in me, and my words abide in you, ask for whatever you wish, and it will be done for you. My Father is glorified by this, that you bear much fruit and become my disciples" (John 15:1–8).

Every thought, every word, every deed, is Jesus' thought, word, and deed. Contemplation at its peak is our being transformed into the image and likeness of Christ or our having obtained the mind of Christ. The old self passes away, and behold all things become new. When we are contemplating at the highest levels, we do not realize exactly what effect our prayers are having, because we have penetrated into the wisdom of God to the point that our intellects cannot contain such lofty knowledge. This is the beauty of the "yes" of Mary. "How can this be?" (Luke 1:34). She couldn't understand but simply said "yes" (Luke 1:38). This is where the contemplative stands; this is where the comatose stand, having received special graces to say "yes," even though they possess no cognitive understanding.

This is exactly where a contemplative person finds himself or herself in the end, saying "yes" to God, sitting and waiting, having no cognitive understanding of where he or she is going or why.

☙ Chapter 3 ❧
Everyone Is a Monk!

Seeking his workman in a multitude of people,
the Lord calls out to him and lifts his voice again:
"Is there anyone here who yearns for life and desires
to see good days?" (Psalms 33[34]:14–15).

RULE OF ST. BENEDICT, PROLOGUE: 14.

L et's reflect some more on what a monk is. A monk is a contemplative person who is suspended between heaven and earth, like Jesus suspended on the cross. He is alive, yet he is dead. Jesus, hanging on the cross, experienced a radical and real detachment from the world. Many may think that the monastic life seems to have no purpose. That is also what is said about those who are chronically ill, aborted, imprisoned, or those who have died sudden and/or tragic deaths. One of the worst things about losing a loved one through any one of these events is that they seem to have no calling or to have fulfilled no purpose. Dare we say that their sudden death, their illness, their imprisonment, their sudden detachment, was their calling? Perhaps it was not only their calling but one of the highest callings attainable in this life, a monastic calling.

If we look at the life of Jesus as the "way," as a path to be followed, we will see events happening in various degrees. Jesus had an apostolic ministry for three years but, as he said to Mary who had "chosen the better part," in the end, he also chose the better part by choosing a monastic calling, the suspension between heaven and earth on the cross (Luke 10:42). Dare we ask about those who were aborted, those who were murdered, those who died from horrible illness, who were imprisoned for life or executed, cut off, as it were, before their time, those who seem to have had no purpose, but instead seem to have died an untimely death—could we possibly begin to see them and ourselves not so much as victims of tragedies, but instead, as a type of heroic martyr? Could we possibly begin to see them and ourselves as Anonymous Monks?

If you have lost a loved one to a violent death, to murder, do not despair. (If you are a person on death row convicted of murder, do not despair.) God has raised such victims up to his eternal glory as martyrs. We can become like them when we are willing to give up all in order to enter into that place where God alone abides.

Try not to worry but rather "pray for yourselves" that you may also live and die as valiantly. Be happy and know that those who have passed away are now enjoying the bliss of heaven, a bliss so great that it no longer remembers the pain of anything on this earth no matter how severe. Please do not doubt that this is true.

Would the good God who holds the power of life and death allow any of these things to happen, especially to his own Son, if this were not the highest of callings: to detach rapidly from the things of this world? Think of the Holy Innocents, all the babies God allowed to be slaughtered when Herod was looking for Jesus (Matthew 2:16). What was their life to God but the purest libation, the purest sacrifice, poured on the altar? What about the victims of the Holocaust? And what about the victims of September 11, 2001 in New York City, Washington, D.C., and Pennsylvania? Do you think that God did not see? Who could dare say that their death was for no purpose, when we know that there is no purer sacrifice than to lay down one's life? (John 15:13) Having said all this, we can now truly say, "Where, O death, is your sting?" (1 Corinthians 15:55).

There is no sting to death, whether the death of a child, of a loved one, or of anyone else because it is "swallowed up in victory," the victory of receiving a high calling, the calling of Anonymous Monk (1 Corinthians 15:55).

✑ Chapter 4 ▧
Falling in Love with Everyone
(A Path to Supreme Happiness)

But as we progress in this way of life and in faith,
we shall run on the path of God's commandments,
our hearts overflowing with the inexpressible delight of love.
RULE OF ST. BENEDICT, PROLOGUE: 49.

Thomas Merton wrote in *Love and Living*: "The question of love is one that cannot be evaded. Whether or not you claim to be interested in it, from the moment you are alive you are bound to be concerned with love, because love is not just something that happens to you: *it is a certain way of being alive.*"

As I grew in the spiritual life, there came a time when I began to be concerned about what I was going to do with my feelings of love, passion, and also illicit sexual attractions. I often would think that perhaps I should suppress my feelings and not allow them to come to the surface. I struggled with questions of who I could love deeply and who I could not love deeply. I worried about feelings that I may not be able to control and so I would often just avoid confronting my feelings, good and bad.

I gave little thought about being loved or loving but rather tried to become pious by being in control of myself. I was very interested in becoming divine but somehow while doing so my development as a human being seemed to be thwarted. In other words, it seemed that in my self-control I was becoming so heavenly that I was of no earthly good, as the saying goes.

I may have been overanalyzing my so-called boundaries with others and because of this I was not opening my heart to everyone as Jesus opens his heart in the images of his Sacred Heart. I seemed to be becoming a prisoner of my own out-of-order desires. I was not sure which desires to retain and which to reject, in what degree, or what fashion.

Then one day, I was watching a video biography of Thomas Merton. The narrator was reading something that Merton had written shortly before he died about the experience that he had at the huge Buddha statues in Polonnaruwa. Merton wrote: "I am able to approach the Buddha barefoot and undisturbed. Then the silence of the extraordinary faces, the great smiles, huge yet subtle, filled with every possibility. Questioning nothing, knowing everything, rejecting nothing. [1]

This statement seemed like such a revelation for me. After I read it, I began to imagine what my relationships might be like if I truly questioned nothing, knew everything, and yet rejected nothing. At that moment it seemed as though a thousand prejudices left me like so many scales falling from my blinded eyes (Acts 9:18).

From that moment, I began to see my acquaintances, family, and neighbors in this openhearted, loving fashion. Suddenly everyone and everything seemed new. One of my neighbors was a teenage boy who had at one time seemed a troublesome young man. With my new eyes he suddenly seemed like such a marvelous creature. The music that he listened to that once seemed loud and abrasive now seemed interesting, as though I had never heard anything like it before. I spent the early part of the evening listening to his music with him and enjoying all the other neighborhood children. In other words, my preconceived judgments that I had accumulated over the years seemed to have vanished, many of which were not my own but had been projected onto me by the negative outlooks of others throughout my life. [2]

All the above happened on the Saturday before Palm Sunday. Later that evening, I went out to dinner with my husband to a restaurant on the beach in Ft. Lauderdale, Florida. As we were driving toward the beach, it seemed as though this revelation of knowing everything, questioning nothing, and rejecting nothing began to blossom into an unusual grace. A deep love for all of humankind was beginning to well up within me.

As we drove, I seemed to be experiencing a much deeper love for my husband than usual. He seemed unusually beautiful and fascinating. I seemed to be listening to him with much greater attentiveness than usual. Our conversation contained an unearthly stark newness. When we arrived at the restaurant, this openness toward all seemed to grow and grow. Everyone that I saw seemed so beautiful. It was though I had never seen human beings before. It reminded me of Jesus' promise, "See, I am making all things new" (Revelation 21:5). Everyone seemed as though they were a unique masterpiece, their hair, their eyes, their mannerisms. I was very intrigued by everyone. I had the awareness that everyone possesses unlimited potential for God's wisdom and knowledge (Psalm 147:5).

I realized how deeply proud God is of every person he has created. I was also proud of every person as any good mother would be of her children. Everyone seemed to belong to me and I realized that in my prayerfulness for the world I had also helped to create them and I was lovingly proud of them and myself.

The waitress that came to our table seemed to be my own sweet daughter and I greeted her with deep love and fondness. I was so impressed with the beauty of everyone that I began to realize how unhappy and unaware of their unique beauty they seemed to be. I felt that this must surely be the way that God sees everyone. I even said to myself that if everyone knew how beautiful they were to God, if everyone knew that he was proud of them, no matter what they had or hadn't done, they would feel lighter than air, supremely happy, and completely forgiven. Then we would say with the psalmist, "I am fearfully and wonderfully made" (Psalm 139:14).

We would know for certain that God's fatherly love for us as his children will never end and that nothing could ever separate us from his love (Romans 8:35). We would be supremely happy. "Happy are those whose transgression is forgiven, whose sin is covered" (Psalm 32:1). Having experienced this tremendous grace, I had found the freedom and joy of being loved and loving others in the deep all-embracing love of the Holy Trinity. I guess you could say that at that moment I truly and deeply loved my neighbor as myself (Matthew 19:19).

What I was feeling seemed to be an echo of Merton's experience at the Buddha statues when he goes on to say: "Looking at these figures, I was suddenly, almost forcibly, jerked clean out of the habitual half-tired vision of things, and an inner clearness, clarity as if exploding from the rocks themselves, became evident and obvious. Surely, with Polonnaruwa my Asian pilgrimage has come clear and purified itself. I mean, I know, and have seen, what I was obscurely looking for." [3]

This is what I now felt. I was no longer taking people for granted or hiding my heart from them. I was beginning to experience the beautiful Christ-like illumination of falling in love with everyone. I had found the intimacy with others that I was seeking.

It seems to me that each one of us is called to fall in love. We are not called to suppress our ability to love but to allow our love to come to the surface and be transformed in Christ. So we are speaking not of suppressing our love but of allowing ourselves to fall in love. We must allow ourselves to fall in love if we are truly seeking to love others as God loves.

In the beginning, when we experience this intense falling in love, we may become fixated on one person. I am not talking about a surface or superficial love. I am talking about the kind of love that is heart-wrenching, anguished desire burning seemingly beyond our control. Yet something is also taking place that is deep, pure, and spiritual.

I wish to make it clear that I am not condoning our fostering thoughts and temptations against chastity. In Christ's Sermon on the Mount Jesus speaks of the severe punishment that awaits us for certain sins left unchecked. Jesus warns us that if we use abusive language we are "liable to judgment" and are in danger of hell (Matthew 5:21–23).

According to Christ, illicit sexual thoughts are just as dangerous to our souls. In the same aforementioned sermon, Jesus warns us that if we even "look" at someone with lust we have already committed an act of adultery in our hearts (Matthew 5:27–30). I am saying this to stress the gravity of sexual sins. Few of us would meditate committing murder and yet, according to Christ, harboring illicit sexual thoughts is equally forbidden and spiritually deadly.

In this chapter, I am suggesting that, if we can work our way through sexual temptations, if in courage and faith and with the grace of God to aid us we go beyond our physical and psychological tendencies, we may find ourselves falling in love, in a Godly sense, with everyone.

When first we experience this deep, often seemingly forbidden love, our only control may be to pray to God and to the Blessed Mother to help us pass through the fire of purification along the path of true love. When the powerful love of God begins to dwell in us we may initially want to think of it as having its climax in an eventual sexual, physical union, but this is simply a natural reflex. This feeling of falling in love unconditionally may happen, and probably will happen, with not just one person, but with many, as we gradually learn to experience deep genuine love with others on all levels.

What we are beginning to realize is that we are falling in love with human beings as such—their beauty, their individual uniqueness. I am in love with all that is human. Oh, beautiful creature that I see standing before me, awesome but vulnerable, magnificent but fallible.

We can learn to drink deeply from the love of others every day, with each person that we meet. Merton also said, "Solitude is a deepening of the present." We learn to gaze intently and to enjoy the person that we are with at any given time. We learn to experience and enjoy deeply the person present before us in the present moment. Oh, earthly beatitude! How exciting it is to truly enjoy each man, to be in love with everyone!

I once had the very good fortune of having a private audience with a bishop. During the entire conversation I sat listening to him intently, admiring and deeply appreciating his humanity, thinking this was human magnificence in all of its splendor. But this same humanity also belongs to criminals, garbage collectors, monks, housewives, alcoholics, addicts, presidents, and prostitutes.

The other human person that I see is woman, woman in all her mystery, in all her majesty. Beautiful! Oh, woman standing before me, unique in beauty and in splendor, without ugliness, without anything gross or undesirable. My love for man, my love for woman, my love for the image of God that together they form—this is my love for God, my supreme happiness.

During those times when I was suppressing my feelings of love, I often became jealous of those who seemed to enjoy loving relationships, especially with the opposite sex. I seemed to be like the elder brother in the biblical story of the prodigal son. In this story we see a young man who loved in the wrong way, who felt an attraction to unite himself with prostitutes.

When the young man came to his senses and decided to return home, his loving father threw a party, while the elder brother was angry. Could it be that the elder brother was jealous of the disordered love that his younger brother had experienced with the prostitutes? The loving father said to the elder brother, "All that I had was already yours." What did the elder brother already have? He had the potential to be truly in love with all people at all times, but he did not realize this and was miserable because of it.

How exciting it is to be falling in love with man, falling in love with woman. Each day is a joy; each person is a joy. All I see is beautiful man, beautiful woman. So allow yourself to fall in love if you have the courage. Try not to suppress your feelings, but allow the Blessed Mother to keep you from trying to limit yourself to a sexual union. Instead, learn to love everyone with a deep spiritual union. Again, Merton, a lover of humankind, steps out in honesty and helps us all.

Anyone who loves God long enough may also find himself or herself wrestling with what I have struggled with, the fountain of God's all-inclusive love welling up from within. As it springs forth, we may direct this universal love to one, two, three, or more persons. After a while, the rivers of living water of God's love for man, God's love for woman, will come bursting through us and we will have the great joy of being madly in love with everyone, every day—truly interested in everyone, every day, interested in their story and their points of view. Like Merton, we will also be interested in other people's religious traditions.

We cannot love freely if we insist on conditions, and if we have to size everyone up before we love them, or if we insist on suppressing true feelings of love dwelling in us (Thomas Merton). I believe that some of Merton's last written words bear witness to all the above. He writes about a woman with whom he shared a deep special love. She is known as M:

I forgot to ask the exact date of her birthday. She was born just about two months before I came through Cincinnati! I had walked through Cincinnati Station with the words of Proverbs, chapter 8 in my mind, "And my delight was to be with the children of men." I had never forgotten this. It struck me forcibly then! Strange connection in my deepest heart between M. and the "wisdom" figure—and Mary—and the feminine in the Bible—Eve, etc.—paradise-wisdom, most mysterious, haunting, deep, lovely, moving, transforming! [4]

In the above text, mature spiritual men and women who have passed beyond their own disordered sexual desires will clearly see that Thomas Merton is merging with M. on a deep spiritual level that goes far beyond any physical union that a man could ever experience with a woman. Merton seems to be experiencing through M. a union with the feminine aspects of the Holy Trinity itself, a union elevated and ecstatic.

How much I love dear Thomas as I write. How much I long to love men and women on this true, honest, and pure level. This type of honesty is humble, painful, and purifying. Perhaps the disordered media and all that it projects into our minds has caused us to look in a sour manner at what is meant to be pure and rich.

The devil knows how powerful this merging with the Holy Trinity is, and he likes to scare us into thinking that to love on this level is forbidden. We may be tempted to believe this lie more readily because we have knowledge of the great trouble and scandal that disordered love can cause. In fact, many of us would rather avoid the vulnerability and lucidity that is required to live at this intimate level of God's truth. And what is this truth but the humility to admit that we wish to love and to be loved at the deepest level of our being, with a love that encompasses the very core of our masculinity and femininity?

Openness to this love is unavoidable. We must eventually allow ourselves, in this life or the next, to love at this depth in order to be absorbed into the very essence of the Holy Trinity. By climbing the heights of humility we shall also receive the great gift that Merton received through his experiences with God in his many years of living the monastic life. We too shall find ourselves on the brink of convergence with the Holy Trinity. "This is my commandment, that you love one another as I have loved you" (John 15:12).

I will end in thanksgiving to Merton for his transparent honesty that helps us all to love deeply and inclusively, and therefore to become true Christians. The Dalai Lama described Merton best when he said of him: "When I think of a Christian, immediately I see his [Thomas Merton's] picture, his vision. I think of a good human being. Deep. A person who has had some deep experience. Not a person who is cheating other people or looking down on people, honest truthful" (*Merton: A Film Biography*).

I place much importance on Thomas Merton's last address in Bangkok. I consider him a martyr for having given his life to deliver it. Not only was Merton a martyr but he was the best kind, because he died alone just as he lived alone. As he has suffered with Christ, so also shall he be glorified (Romans 8:17). Therefore, in my opinion, Thomas Merton died a saint and is worthy of possible canonization by the authorities of the Roman Catholic Church. Ordinary people, especially those who have suffered, those who are suffering now, and those who will suffer great humiliations in future generations for the sake of obtaining the truth need to know where the Catholic Church officially stands in regard to this beautiful man of God. Then without question or concern the whole of humankind, the ignorant and the learned, can embrace him and his teachings unreservedly.

I consider this book an extension of Thomas Merton's life and work because in faithfulness to God he persevered in monastic life. This ultimately led him to deliver that final message in Bangkok where he strongly exhorted ordinary persons in the spirit of the call to holiness to stand on their own feet.

1. *Intimate Merton*, p. 361.
2. Thomas Merton,*The Inner Experience*, p. 1.
3. *Intimate Merton*, p. 362.
4. *Intimate Merton*, pp. 301–302.

⚝ Chapter 5 ⚝

Experiencing Solitude in All Circumstances

Place your hope in God alone.
RULE OF ST. BENEDICT, 4:41.

Solitude is not just a place but a state of mind and heart. With solitude comes the realization that we have a unique calling that no one else can fulfill. When in humility and obedience we accept the challenge of our unique vocation we will eventually realize that we are on a path that is narrow and where there is no one else but God and ourselves.

Our individual path is as unique as our fingerprints. There are no two paths exactly alike. If we stay on our unique path and accept it as such we will have discovered true solitude. As we strive to fulfill our unique vocation we must accept that we will not be able to lean on anyone or anything but Christ. Like Peter departing on the waves, we go alone. We must depart. This is solitude.

Like Mary and Joseph in the stable of Christ's birth, we find ourselves alone with Christ and empathizing with the nature of plants and animals. No one can truly feel our feelings or have deep knowledge of our thoughts but God. This realization is solitude. We must go it alone. To enter into solitude we must accept the hidden interior challenges of our lives. In our joyful acceptance, we have become martyrs of sorts in our solitude.

Centuries ago there were monks known as stylites. They lived on the top of pillars or platforms as representatives of the narrow way to God. [1] Solitude is like this in the sense that there seems to be very little room for pride without our falling away from true interior solitude. The devil will try to pick us off, so to speak, through individuals who try to capture our attention, often by accusations, insults, and unreasonable demands. People will want everything we may possess, our money, our clothes, anything of value that they think we care about.

To remain on the pillar of solitude we must remember the words of Christ, "If anyone wants to sue you and take your coat, give your cloak as well; and if anyone forces you to go one mile, go also the second mile. Give to everyone who begs from you, and do not refuse anyone who wants to borrow from you" (Matthew 5:40–42).

Truly living for God in this way cannot be feigned. We must descend into the depths of humility and heed Christ's words, "Do this in remembrance of me" (Luke 22:19), in the memory of the all-powerful God who mounted the cross and still had the wherewithal to utter, "Father, forgive them; for they do not know what they are doing" (Luke 23:34). This attitude of complete interior and exterior renunciation must be lived in order to experience true and lasting solitude.

When we are tempted to defend ourselves because of pride we can stop and reflect and know that we are about to give up our great gift of solitude. Most likely we should remain courteous and silent. When we have no answer for our enemies we become like Christ before Pilate. Christ "who gave him no answer" (John 19:9).

We can remember that the Kingdom of God is not about food or drink, clothes, money, accusations, hate crimes, or anything else "but righteousness and peace and joy in the Holy Spirit" (Romans 14:17). As Anonymous Monks let us remain in the happiness of heaven. This is the solitude of the Anonymous Monk, the place in which we dwell.

As Anonymous Monks we may experience a heightened sense of our aloneness with God because few persons have knowledge of our struggles or advancements in Christ. We have no monastery, elaborate liturgies, or religious garb to cling to or to hide behind. We must stand before God naked and unattached. Our strong belief in prayer is made evident when we resist the temptation to get involved in disputes about material possessions and with the conflicts and mood swings of others. In prayer we remain hidden and effective like the angels, Mary the Mother of God, and the saints who have gone before us.

With God's grace to aid us, we must possess the courage of Saint Maximilian Kolbe. He was a Catholic priest who was taken by the Gestapo to a Nazi concentration camp. While there he volunteered to die in the place of another prisoner. He was stripped of his clothing and left to die in the starvation bunker. [2] As Anonymous Monks we are stripped down interiorly, and often exteriorly, to the bare essentials.

1. *Catholic Encyclopedia*, p. 1226.
2. *My Sunday Bulletin*, St. Francis de Sales Press.

❧ Chapter 6 ❧

Is Marriage for You?

With his good gifts which are in us, we must obey him
at all times that he may never become the angry father
who disinherits his sons, nor the dread lord,
enraged by our sins, who punishes us forever
as worthless servants for refusing to follow him to glory.
RULE OF ST. BENEDICT, PROLOGUE: 6.

Since, by the grace of God, you happen to be reading this book, there is a possibility that you may be called to live as a monk or nun in a monastery. That is why I have written this chapter. "Let anyone with ears listen!" (Matthew 13:43).

The higher purpose of marriage is that each spouse helps to lead the other to God. Not everyone needs a spouse to draw nearer to God. For many persons, marriage would be a distraction from God. Some holy persons, however, feel that together with their spouse they can do the work of God.

What many do not realize is that in either situation, whether married or unmarried, each vocation has for its interior goal the total devotion of the self to God. Jesus says, "Whoever comes to me and does not hate father and mother, wife and children, brothers and sisters, yes, and even life itself, cannot be my disciple" (Luke 14:26). Paul urges the people of Corinth: "Let even those who have wives be as though they had none" (1 Corinthians 7:29). In other words, that no person, spouse, or child take the place of our God.

Let's remember Paul's words:

> I want you to be free from anxieties. The unmarried
> man is anxious about the affairs of the Lord, how to

please the Lord; but the married man is anxious about the affairs of the world, how to please his wife, and his interests are divided. And the unmarried woman and the virgin are anxious about the affairs of the Lord, so that they may be holy in body and spirit; but the married woman is anxious about the affairs of the world, how to please her husband. I say this for your own benefit, not to put any restraint upon you, but to promote good order and unhindered devotion to the Lord (1 Corinthians 7:32–35).

Paul is telling us and perhaps even warning us of the hardships and responsibility of marriage and family. Paul admits that it can be quite difficult to serve God wholeheartedly with a spouse and family. This is why persons with religious careers are usually single and celibate, as was Jesus, John the Baptist, and most of the saints. This should speak volumes to us about the power of virginity.

It is sometimes hard to understand why very holy persons struggle with whether or not they should get married, when it is obvious that they are well on their way to God without a spouse. Furthermore, this book does not even begin to speak of the great benefits of the celibate life, how energy not wasted, including sexual energy, is infused directly into the service of God.

God allows this type of temptation. What good is devotion that cannot be tested? In other words, it is easy to stay celibate when no suitable partner is available, but when the person of one's dreams stands directly in sight and one stays devoted to God, this is when real devotion is made evident. Temptations of this type show the persons who have them whether or not they have a disordered will. A person whose will is in proper order is not moved by temptation because one must want the sin in order to be moved by it.

Remember, Scripture says that "whatever does not proceed from faith is sin" (Romans 14:23). Therefore, if one can honestly say that they marry in faith, then they should. Or if in faith they stay celibate, they should. Whatever is harder usually takes faith.

There is the case when the Lord does ask a person to marry a particular person in order to lead them both to salvation in God. If a person hears the voice of God within, asking him or her to devote his or her life to the salvation of one person through marriage, then that person should respond to God's call, by prayer, service, and a strong faith in eternal life.

Anonymous Monks in marriage should be committed to the eternal salvation of their spouse. God loves each soul so much that Christ would have come to earth even if there were only one person. Recall how Joseph was planning to dismiss Mary privately when he found out that she was pregnant. Then he changed his mind, because God had asked him to marry her. This is the truest reason to marry anyone—because God asks us to.

H aving said all this, we should recall the beautiful story of Heloise and Abelard. Abelard was madly in love with Heloise, but Heloise loved Abelard so much that she refused to marry him. She was convinced that he was a man who belonged to the world and was too good for just one woman. Heloise exhibited a sacrificial love, while Abelard had a love that sought pleasure for itself by the possession of Heloise. Just as Mary gave up Jesus to die on the cross, sometimes true love means letting a person go to do the work God has for them, even if that work does not include us.

Jesus said, "Truly I tell you, there is no one who has left house or brothers and sisters or mother or father or children or fields, for my sake and for the sake of the good news, who will not receive a hundredfold now in this age" (Mark 10:29). This means we must broaden our minds and our perspective concerning the abundance of God. Like a good father, God never asks us to give anything up without giving us something much better.

When we live for God everyone truly becomes our mother, brother, father, son, and daughter. I am speaking of a very deep spiritual bond. In time, and with the help of God's grace, we learn to love on a deep spiritual level that is profoundly satisfying. We come to know others as they truly are. We also come to know ourselves and to be ourselves. We truly love others and ourselves as the beautiful and intelligent creatures that we are.

Jesus said, "'Who is my mother? Who are my brothers?' And pointing to his disciples, he said, 'Here are my mother and my brothers! For whoever does the will of my Father in heaven is my brother and sister and mother'" (Matthew 12:48–50). It is truly earthly beatitude when we experience this deep spiritual kinship with everyone, every day. What joy! What happiness!

Becoming a monk, nun, priest, brother, or sister is an exciting challenge, whereby we can excel in self-mastery and advance in the science of love. The opportunities for self-discovery are endless.

All types of persons are needed—carpenters, doctors, nurses, handymen, typists, mechanics, writers, those with education and those with none. The employment in a religious community is plentiful, secure, and varied. A person who is free to enter a monastery, a seminary, or a religious community should seek to join if he or she is acceptable as a candidate. And the only way to know is to actually try it and see how it goes.

The freedom to enter such a community is in itself a great providential gift from God. I am primarily speaking of those who are unmarried and free from the obligation to care for others as with young children and aged parents and in reasonably good physical and mental health. One must also be relatively free from debt.

▨ Chapter 7 ▧
Stop Acting Like an Animal

"Do not gratify the promptings of the flesh"
(Galatians 5:16); hate the urgings of self-will.
RULE OF ST. BENEDICT, 4:59–60.

The next five chapters are meant to lay down a foundation of love. Until we become willing to love others as ourselves, and brush away our desire to cling to the past or to bitterness, we will not be in a position to live out the monastic practices and reflections outlined.

The degree to which Anonymous Monks are ruled by their senses (the animal man) [1] is the degree to which we are not yet wholly spiritual. What do we mean by "animal" versus "spiritual" man? Throughout the Anonymous Monk's day, the flesh is laboring against the spirit (Romans 8:22). Every time God makes a move to speak to us with his divine wisdom, we have some knee-jerk reaction, some vice rears its ugly head. God is moving in the soul to speak to us, and as he does, our bodies can hardly resist the temptation clinging to our animal instincts.

The animal instinct is to do something primal, such as getting something to eat, having a drink of alcohol, smoking a cigarette, eating some candy, watching television, going shopping—anything other than turning toward God and listening. Little do we realize that if we fought the good fight of faith just a little longer, that is to say, if we would call out to Jesus for strength, God would reveal to us some very pertinent direction for virtuous living. Just like the married couple who makes it to the counselor, or the family who goes to church together, healing in some fashion takes place.

When our soul has freed itself by God's grace from every vice, then we are truly ready to do God's work. Now, when we move, it is God moving in us, because the Spirit of God is no longer being quenched by our animal instincts. The more we continually resist the desires of the flesh, the more we are able to hear from God, i.e., the more spiritually directed we become. If we insist on hanging on to the desires of the flesh, we will never know the good that we have not accomplished. It is scary to realize that major works of God are not being accomplished because of our clinging to something as insignificant as a cigarette, fine clothing, a prestigious position in life.

The Bible contains many instances where persons suffered major spiritual loss over little things. Consider the story of Adam and Eve, how the parents of all of humankind fell over an apple. Adam and Eve chose to receive gratification from sensual things rather than attending to the things of God. It really is a serious matter, because gratifying the senses is actually a sign of spiritual death to some degree (Genesis 3:3). Let's also remember the story of Esau, who sold his birthright for a bowl of stew (Genesis 25:31).

The problem is not things but resting in things, instead of resting in God. Anonymous Monks use things, food, clothes, money, cars, for the purposes for which they were made. It is when we glory in sensual things rather than in God that the work of the spirit is stifled.

The purpose of any spiritual rulebook is to help people to develop the life of God within them. They do so by aiding us in adhering to certain disciplines and practices, practices that offer the maximum potential for remaining free from vice (death) and growing in virtue (life).

As Anonymous Monks, not only do we ourselves grow spiritually, but we believe that by our practices many others grow with us. Conversely, as with Adam and Eve, when we fall so do many others. Many persons are gracefully sustained because of our commitment to these monastic practices. We should not underestimate the power of a prayerful monastic life. Let us not get weary but like runners running a race let us endure to the end. When we reach the Kingdom of God, then we will realize the full importance of our disciplines.

1. *The Golden Epistle*, p. 25.

≋ Chapter 8 ≋
Breaking Free from Bad Habits

Do not aspire to be called holy before you really are,
but first be holy that you may more truly be called so.
RULE OF ST. BENEDICT, 4:62.

≋A nonymous Monks progressively seek to rest in peace, that is to say, to rest in God, to the point that we are resting in God alone. Not that we don't enjoy things. We enjoy things even more when we can use them for what they are and without clinging to them. This is the ultimate lesson everyone must learn. God is the very essence of all good things. By letting go of vice, we learn truly to enjoy God in everything.

Unbelief is the continual hanging on to vices. Many of us fear that there is nothing beyond the present sensual stimulus to which we are addicted. We fear that the things we have, the things we cling to, may be taken away.

In actuality, we will discover that, by letting go of vices, we travel deeper into faith. Our faith will lead us to the truth that we can live beyond our senses in the realm of joy in the spirit. It is much like the crucifixion and the resurrection. The painful crucifixion of vices, eventually, is transformed into the joy of resurrected virtue. This moving from vice to virtue is a foretaste of our eternal resurrection with Jesus.

The crucifying of vices can be painful. The deeper our attachment to something, the more painful it is to let it die. The type of sensual things that we rest in varies greatly from individual to individual. Some of us may rest in having a particular type of clothing, hairstyle, status in the community, a particular paycheck at the end of the week, food, and so on. Some of us may have to let go of relationships that are hurting or holding back our spiritual progress. This detaching can be very painful.

If we look at the amount of energy at our disposal as a pie, and if we divide this pie into various slices that represent our habits and fondness for things, we will get a clear picture of where we are expending our energies. We have to remember that when we take time and energy away from vices, we have this much more time and energy left for virtue. Spending less time and energy loving things equates to having more time and energy for loving God. This insight follows the saying, "No pain, no gain." When we strive to love God with our whole heart at all times, the more we progress, the more we use our time and energy efficiently.

Eliminating any vice can bring on a feeling of emptiness known as the "void." [1] The void is the suffering that comes because energy once used for vice has not yet been rerouted to virtue. We can feel irritable and depressed, like a small child whose pacifier has been taken away. However, if we have the courage to endure the void, we will eventually discover that God has rerouted and transformed our energy to a habit that is virtuous. Being virtuous it is now eternal, not temporal as with vice. With the crucifixion of vice, in time, one will certainly feel the joy of the resurrection of virtue.

When Anonymous Monks become aware of how they have grown in virtue, they experience great joy and are filled with thanksgiving for this new gift. We discover that the vice that we considered so important was merely an illusion of false worldly joy.

By systematically moving from vice to virtue, we become a better and better receptacle for divine wisdom. Gradually, our minds become Christ's minds and our bodies become Christ's bodies. This is why Jesus said to Martha and Mary that Mary had chosen the better part and that it would not be "taken away from her" (Luke 10:42). The better part was to put all her energy into the enjoyment of God. It is exciting to know that what we have, this constant attentiveness to God, can and will never be taken away from us. Jesus promises us that we will continually enjoy a God that is infinite and eternal.

So we realize that vice is temporary and dies, whereas virtue is eternal and gives life forever. By rerouting the energy used for vice to grow in virtue and enter into Jesus' presence, who came that we "may have life and have it abundantly" (John 10:10).

1. *Collected Works of St. John of the Cross*, p. 122.

≋ Chapter 9 ≋
Healing Bad Memories

"I am bowed down and humbled in every way"
(Psalms 37 [38]:7–9. Psalms 118 [119]:107).
RULE OF ST. BENEDICT, 7:66.

The memory is made up of objects and events impressed upon the mind through the senses. Negative events can traumatize the memory. Physiologically, it could be explained like this. As Anonymous Monks gradually become more wholly spiritual by not resting in sensual (animal) delights, the trauma of memory seems gradually to erase. It is the reverse of what seems to happen to amnesia victims. An amnesia victim can experience a sudden trauma and have absolutely no memory of his family, his life, or even who he is. If he smells a certain smell or hears a certain sound, however, the memory can be jarred. [1] So again, when the process is reversed, when the senses are cut off, they dry up and are forgotten, leaving nothing for the memory to hang on to.

A person going through this mental purgation is experiencing the beginnings of preparation for receiving the mind of Christ. Memories of one's own sinfulness and the reality of what one has done flood the mind like pus oozing from an infected wound. During this phase a person must really think carefully about mending past wrongs. If one can apologize or make amends for past evil deeds, one should. For it is doubtful that one can progress to true healing of the mind and memory without at least being willing to make amends. This means that if someone has committed evil deeds in the past they should come clean to the proper persons.

Writing a letter, for example, to explain that you have changed your evil ways and are sorry, will bring a healing that is well worth the humiliation of the truth. Paying back money owed, to the best of one's ability, will begin to bring about healing. If the persons harmed have died, or cannot be found, a person should do good to their family, as did David with Saul's family in the Old Testament (2 Samuel 9).

We should make an honest review of our conscience, and allow ourselves to bare everything in the open to achieve a complete healing. We must place everything on the altar, to be burnt up as a holocaust acceptable to God. As a physician deals with the body, so memories cannot be healed if a person is not willing to disclose what is wrong.

One who is willing to make amends insofar as it is possible will also experience a greater awareness of the evils of others. In order to receive complete healing, God wishes all to follow Jesus' example. Jesus had full knowledge of the evils perpetrated against him and was still willing to forgive and pray for all (Luke 23:34). God is preparing the individual to receive the mind of Christ. The old mind with the old baggage and trauma of memories is not able to receive the mind of Christ (1 Corinthians 2:16). It is the story of old wineskins incapable of receiving new wine without bursting (Luke 5:37).

The mind, including the memory, must be rejuvenated. Persons going through this rejuvenation process could experience extreme bouts of memory loss. [2] Eventually, the memory returns but it is a fresh, pure, born-again memory (John 3:3). With this healing of the memory, an Anonymous Monk, probably for the first time, uses his or her senses in the way that God originally intended. He or she still has memories, but all past events, negative and positive, are seen as having worked out for good. There is no trauma attached to past memories. A person is so detached from the pain of his or her own bad memories that events remembered seem almost to have happened to someone else—and indeed they did, they happened to the old self.

Healing of the memory brings to mind the Old Testament story of Joseph who was sold as a slave by his brothers (his senses). Having spent many years in prison (in sensory deprivation), Joseph was eventually released (became wholly spiritual), and God exalted him in order to save his brothers and others. Joseph came to realize that God was at work all along throughout the seemingly negative years (Genesis 37ff). The trauma of the memory was erased because he realized that everything that had happened bore meaning and purpose. Joseph experienced the true freedom of the children of God (Genesis 50:19–21).

1. *Understanding Catholic Christianity*, p. 62.
2. *The Collected Works of St. John of the Cross*, p. 269.

৯ Chapter 10 ৮

Dealing Gracefully with People

"They should try to be the first to show respect
to the other" (Romans 12:10), supporting with the greatest
patience one another's weaknesses of body and behavior,
and earnestly competing in obedience to one another.
RULE OF ST. BENEDICT, 72:4.

T he Trinity is undivided unity. [1] To the degree that we experience malicious division from others, to this same degree are we divided and separated from God. We cannot expect to enter into the fullness of God, beatitude, as long as malicious division still exists on our part.

If as Anonymous Monks we experience unresolved malicious division, we must seek to reconcile with every person to the best of our ability, now, in this life. With holy fear, we should remember the Scripture passage, "So when you are offering your gift at the altar, if you remember that your brother or sister has something against you, leave your gift there before the altar and go; first be reconciled to your brother or sister, and then come and offer your gift" (Matthew 5:23–24).

In heaven there is a complete absence of malicious division. Recalling the Lord's Prayer, "Your kingdom come. Your will be done, on earth as it is in heaven" (Matthew 6:10), one may ask how this unity of the kingdom is to be achieved here on earth. It is achieved by the practice of the Lord's Prayer where further Jesus says, "And forgive us our debts, as we also have forgiven our debtors" (Matthew 6:12).

Anonymous Monks strive to forgive all so that they themselves and those who have offended them do not have to undergo the pain of reconciling division in this life or the next. If we have unintentionally offended someone, we should still apologize, not necessarily for having done anything wrong but simply for having offended our neighbor. The Anonymous Monk should be willing to be the first one to undergo the humility of reconciliation out of love for God and neighbor.

Like Jesus, Anonymous Monks are willing to take the blame. We forgive, and by our humility we atone for the sins of many, remembering the words of Isaiah, "The righteous one, my servant, shall make many righteous, and he shall bear their iniquities . . . because he poured out himself to death and was numbered with the transgressors; yet he bore the sin of many and made intercession for the transgressors" (Isaiah 53:11b–12).

Furthermore, Jesus said, "Whatever you bind on earth will be bound in heaven, and whatever you loose on earth will be loosed in heaven" (Matthew 18:18). In this way, we free our offenders from the future pain of purgation of malicious division.

The importance of reconciliation should not be underrated, remembering Jesus' warning, "Come to terms quickly with your accuser. . . . [Y]ou will never get out [of prison] until you have paid the last penny" (Matthew 5:25–26). By "forgiving those who trespass against them," Anonymous Monks respond to the words of Isaiah: "Prepare the way of the Lord" so that "the crooked shall be made straight and the rough ways made smooth," and "all flesh shall see the salvation of God" (Luke 3:6). We do this for the sake of the Kingdom, for the sake of undivided unity, for the sake of the Holy Trinity. "How very good and pleasant it is when kindred live together in unity" (Psalm 133:1).

In view of the above, as Anonymous Monks it is important for us to stay on good terms with all persons, at all times. Being at peace with others enforces our union with God. Others are for us a source of contact with God. As Scripture says, "Those who say, 'I love God,' and hate their brothers or sisters, are liars" (1 John 4:20). This includes salespersons, neighbors, strangers—everyone.

Being kind and hospitable is a form of prayer, if we do so for the love of God. We all have many opportunities for kindness and hospitality each day. Welcoming strangers and door-to-door salespeople can be an opportunity for prayer.

An Anonymous Monk who lives in a well-lit and populated area should greet salespeople and strangers with absolute kindness in speech and manners, looking at each of them as though they were "Christ himself." [2] Anonymous Monks who can afford it might even try to buy a little something from all salespeople (especially children). To do so is a mark of respect and kindness to the seller more than esteem for the product. Perhaps, if we cannot purchase anything, we could at least give a small donation or an encouraging word. The encouraging word applies especially to salespersons who may call us on the telephone.

If we are home alone, or with children, we should speak outside on the porch, or in the front yard, out of safety considerations. If our children need our attention, we should kindly say so and close the door. (At no time should we ever place our children or those in our household at risk, simply to answer the door.)

If an Anonymous Monk lives in a secluded area, for safety's sake we may wish to use caution welcoming strangers and possibly not even answer the door.

1. *Christian Prayer*, p. 1597.
2. *Rule of St. Benedict*, 53:1.

⊗ Chapter 11 ⊗

Revenge Is Wrong

No one is to pursue what he judges better for himself,
but instead, what he judges better for someone else.
RULE OF ST. BENEDICT, 72:7.

Every human being has innate importance and supreme value. As Anonymous Monks we strive to truly love all persons without having to judge whether or not they deserve our love or if they are in God's grace.

I believe that inside of every human being is that which always was, that which was uncreated, that which we call God. These truths are the very foundation of justice. In other words, justice provides a code of conduct that says every man, woman, and child should be treated with respect, regardless of their outward appearance, regardless of behavior, simply because they exist.

In Sacred Scripture we hear of Jesus hanging on the cross, looking over the angry mob, and praying, "Father, forgive them; for they do not know what they are doing" (Luke 23:34). What outward sign of worthiness did any one of those condemning Jesus to death show? There was none. What did Jesus see as he hung on the cross that would prompt him sincerely to pray for them? Jesus saw in each person, in the core of their very being, this uncreated presence which is God, the triune God, the Holy Trinity, three persons and yet one in "being." [1]

So, when Jesus saw God in the angry crowd and prayed for them, he was actually praying for the God in them to be united with the God in himself. In other words, Jesus was loving them simply because they existed or better put, simply because God existed in them. Thomas Merton wrote: "The charity of the saint, which is sanctity, is nothing else but God's sanctity mirrored in the saint. God's love for himself, mirrored in a fallen and redeemed creature, becomes God's mercy for man. And so the love of the saint for God is at the same time God's love for himself, God's love for the saint, and God's love for mankind." [2]

According to justice, an Anonymous Monk should "render each person his or her due." [3] And what is his or her due? That each man, each women, and each child be respected, that each one be revered, because inside of every one is that which is uncreated, that which is God. Anyone who sincerely thinks like this is close to perfect unity with the Holy Trinity itself.

Remember the many stories in the *Sayings of the Desert Fathers* where we read of heroic kindness and submission shown to those who did not merit it. Let us also remember the many sayings of Jesus, words like: "Love your enemies and pray for those who persecute you" (Matthew 5:44). "Love your enemies, do good to those who hate you" (Luke 6:27). "Whoever wants to be first must be last of all and servant of all" (Mark 9:35). "All who exalt themselves will be humbled, and all who humble themselves will be exalted" (Matthew 23:12).

Scripture is full of this type of justice, this type of humility. I am saying all of this because, until we learn how to love, our monastic practices will be powerless and meaningless.

1. Nicene Creed.
2. *Disputed Questions*, p. 28.
3. *Catholic Encyclopedia*, p. 726.

Chapter 12

Structuring Our Prayer Life

*The Prophet says: "Seven times a day
shall I praise you" (Psalms 118 [119]:164).*

RULE OF ST. BENEDICT, 16:1.

I n this chapter, I cover the various prayers that have become the
foundation of our lives. The Psalms are the heart of the Liturgy
of the Hours, also known as the Breviary or the Divine Office. Praying
the Psalms is considered a more perfect way of praying because we are
praying the sacred Word of God to God. Monks usually pray the Divine
Office (Psalms) seven times a day.

As Anonymous Monks, we strive to make praying an important
priority. Nothing in this life should be preferred to taking time to stop and
pray. [1] Let us try to say three Psalms at each time of prayer. (There is a
section in the back of this book explaining how to pray the Psalms for
those who are interested.) But, if we do not have a copy of the Psalms,
then we can feel free to make good use of whatever prayers we have
available even if we have to make them up ourselves. The important thing
is that we make time to calm ourselves and to heighten our awareness
that God is constantly watching us and is aware of all our actions.

Why am I saying this? Because when we break for prayer, not only
are we centering ourselves in God, but we are also refocusing our mental
energies. By taking time to pray, all of our activities will become more
effective. By channeling our energies, we become a better receptacle for
receiving and participating in God's creative power. We need not rack
our brains all day trying to think of better ways to do the tasks required
of us. It takes a lot less effort to actually "do" God's work than it does to
do what we think is God's work.

We should strive to pray at least seven times daily [2] in a subtle manner, not drawing any undue attention to ourselves. If we add up all the time that it takes to pray the Psalms, it only amounts to a little over an hour. In the time that it takes to smoke a cigarette, we could be drawing energy from the source of all life through prayer.

Forming the good habit of praying throughout our day may take time. We should start off slowly, maybe praying only once a day for a few months. Then after a while, we can build up to two times a day, etc. We have to be careful not to take on too much at once, because we don't want to run the risk of overburdening ourselves and giving up completely.

Spiritual exercises are the same as physical exercises in that if we try to run the Boston Marathon the first day or even the first year, we will most likely drop out. We should try to use prudence if we are going to endure faithfully in a lifetime of prayer. This is a way of living, not a fad or a New Year's resolution that vanishes when the novelty wears off.

We must be realistic about what we are able to do and not fall into the habit of just having to complete goals, even prayerful goals. In time, our schedule for prayer could look something like this:

Early morning prayer	6:00 A.M.
Morning prayer	9:00 A.M.
Midmorning prayer	10:00 A.M.
Midday prayer	12:00 noon
Midafternoon prayer	3:00 P.M.
Evening prayer	5:30 P.M.
Nighttime prayer	8:00 P.M.

Those who are able to begin their early morning prayer while it is still dark should. Praying in the early morning before sunrise has long been a monastic practice. We believe that God is present in the sunlight. Jesus, like the sun, sheds the light of truth within our hearts. So, while it is dark, we can meditate on the Son of God rising for the salvation of a world in darkness.

We can also remember that a monk, like the sun, dwells in silence, but still, like the sun, his presence is felt throughout the world. Likewise, your time of praying the evening prayer should be around sunset, if possible, for the same reasons mentioned above.

Try not to forgo praying the Psalms for any reason. In order to breathe spiritually, we must pray the Psalms regularly. If for some reason we miss a time of prayer, we should not worry about it. Just skip it and pray at the next time of prayer, if possible.

Even when we are extremely busy, we can usually recite something by heart. For example, we might pray silently as we walk across the parking lot. We can usually recite some Psalm or prayer from memory. If a Psalm does not come to mind, we can say an Our Father, Hail Mary, or simply the words, "Jesus, save us," or "Jesus," or "God, help us," or simply, "God." (The Hail Mary, the Our Father, the Angelus, and directions on how to pray the Rosary are printed in the back of this book.)

When we are able to stop for prayer, we can sometimes pray more discreetly by stepping aside to a restroom or to our car. Often, the Psalms can be said on a bus, in a waiting room, as we stand in line in the cafeteria, or at the park while the children play. It may be necessary to photocopy portions of the Psalms, such as the gradual Psalms, 120–134, so that we can pray in public more discreetly.

For some of us, it may be better to say the same Psalms at the same time each day. Through repetition, we will then memorize those Psalms and be able to go about our tasks while reciting them in our minds. (Also, for those of you in prison, it may be a good idea to memorize the Psalms, in the event that your Bible is stolen or taken away.)

Those of us who are blessed with additional time can also pray the Angelus, the Rosary, or simply say the words "Jesus, save me a sinner." So, as you see, the foundation of our prayer life is the Psalms. In between Psalms, we can pray the Angelus, the Rosary, or utter quick prayers throughout our day. If we continue on this high calling of constant prayer we shall indeed "pray without ceasing." This does not mean that we should ignore people, but that, when possible, when our thoughts are not busy with the concerns of this world, we can busy ourselves with thoughts that turn our hearts toward God. (Those who are too sick to read, should try to arrange to have prayers read to them or played on cassette.)

In the end, each Anonymous Monk's prayer life will be different. Each person will have adjusted his or her schedule for prayer, according to the opportunities that the Lord provides.

Let us not pressure ourselves to accomplish prayers for the sake of getting them done, but instead, let us dip from the well whenever we feel that we need refreshment. Prayer will be our refreshment for the purpose of remaining kind, patient, humble, charitable, and seeing every person we meet as another self, as Christ himself, refreshment not only for ourselves but for the whole world.

1. *Rule of St. Benedict*, 48:22–23.
2. "Statute on Unity and Pluralism," 1969, *Trappist Guidelines*, #3.

🥨 Chapter 13 🥨

Finding God
in Our Daily Work

First of all, every time you begin a good work, you must
pray to [Jesus] most earnestly to bring it to perfection.

RULE OF ST. BENEDICT, PROLOGUE: 4.

🥨A nonymous Monks who are healthy should work (2 Thessalonians 3:10). Work is an opportunity to participate in God's creation and restoration, remembering that Christ also worked as a carpenter. Also, hard work is a means of self-support and exercises our mind and body. [1]

Working can also take the edge off of our constant prayer schedule and provide a broader, more informal "hands on" type of prayer. For instance, if we pick up litter, we can believe that we are participating in God's restoration by restoring the area to cleanliness. If we are spooning out food in the kitchen, we can see ourselves as Jesus feeding the multitudes. If we are in the medical field, we can see ourselves as participating in the healing ministry of Christ. If we are lawyers, we can see ourselves as seekers of truth and justice.

This approach to work can be difficult at first. I found that I had to be willing to let go of all the things that I was addicted to before I could see things afresh. I literally had to go back to the beginning of my self. I had to let go of the idea of finding my identity in fame, fortune, or beauty in order to find my true identity, my true self. I had to start with a clean slate, so to speak. Over time, I had to let go of the little things as well, things that I did habitually like drinking coffee every morning, buying clothes I didn't need, primping myself daily and glorying in my beauty.

These things may not be bad in themselves, but if I didn't have them each day, I was left feeling depressed, like the rich young nobleman who went away sad.

The truth of the matter is that God alone should have been enough to keep me from being depressed. Unfortunately, when it came right down to it, my possessions were all that I was not willing to let go of. They were, in a sense, my idols. I had to have my stuff. I had to pay these things homage every day. In reality, these things were holding me hostage. It may sound as if I am making too much of little things, but I have heard that it was said by Saint John of the Cross, that it doesn't matter what is holding a bird down—be it a silk thread or a heavy chain.

I did not realize that, once I went without my disordered desires, I would experience a rebirth of sorts into another dimension, a dimension where, like a baby, everything seemed new. God had spread a table before me in the desert of self-deprivation, a table where I could then see with supernatural eyes things that I was too distracted to notice before. I had been too distracted by my habits to be in the present moment. I was in my moment, the moment that said, "I am going to get my coffee in the morning if it kills me." Or "I am going to be better than anyone else in whatever I do, whether it is the will of God or not." You see, I wasn't totally open to God because I had a good part of my day already programmed with my bad habits.

In contrast now, every moment is fresh. Peeling an orange, using a computer, sweeping the floor—these are exciting, as though it were the first time. In this process, we truly become like a little child where everything is fun and fascinating. This is the way work becomes. Like a child wanting to help its mother with everything, we look forward to jumping into the present moment wholeheartedly, no matter what the task—baking bread, teaching students in a classroom, doing health-care work, cleaning the cat box. Whether these tasks are challenging or something that I can naturally do well, if they are not performed perfectly all of the time, they are masterpieces to me and to God, because we did them together, with the gifts that God has given me.

This joy we experience is the purest form of thanksgiving. Other people may be breathing down our necks to perform each task with superhuman perfection, but we must resist the temptation to allow our peace to be destroyed by the disordered expectations of those who just want to look good in front of their boss or neighbors at our expense. For now, we hope to recollect ourselves throughout each task, mindful that we should try not to go beyond what we can do in peace. Christ is the Prince of Peace, and he said, "I leave you peace, my peace I give you."

Over time, with the help of God's grace, there comes a great point of conscious transformation when our minds, now renewed, can relate every action, every sight, every sound, to some aspect of the life of Jesus. This is when even our sight, sound, touch, and taste are aware of the presence of Christ without our thinking about it or figuring it with our minds. This is very exciting when we truly see that Christ is in all, for all. For example, I once heard of a person who, having heard water dripping from the leaves of a tree, understood it as the droplets of Christ's blood hitting the ground during his crucifixion on the tree. If we are sitting in a wooden chair we can remember the wood on which Christ was crucified. When we see the sun rise, we see the resurrection of Christ, the one who sheds the light of truth on the whole world.

If we are being yelled at or cursed, we can imagine ourselves as Jesus hanging on the cross in front of an angry mob yelling, "Crucify him!" (I must add that after a while even insults seem sweet. We begin to understand that all men and women are human and have weaknesses. Just as the child having a temper tantrum needs comfort, we realize that hostility is often a cry for help.) I believe that the angry mob at the foot of the cross represented humanity on the brink of hopelessness, their hearts crying out "God, save us!" while their mouths were spewing insults. Let us pray to God for the gift of understanding.

In all work, in all situations, we understand every action as being in Christ and for Christ, with gratitude, thanksgiving, and respect. In this way, we can gain a better understanding of how each of us is so very important to God, as if we were the only person on earth. God never takes his eyes off us. He literally surrounds us with good things. Let us then return so great an attentiveness by remaining aware of God and his goodness in all things, especially our work.

1. *Trappist Constitution*, ch. 26.

Chapter 14

Finding God
When We Read

*On Sunday all are to be engaged in reading except those who
have been assigned various duties. If anyone is so remiss
and indolent that he is unwilling or unable to study or read,
he is to be given some work in order that he may not be idle.*

RULE OF ST. BENEDICT, 48:22.

⊠T he Holy Spirit has knowledge of everything that exists. This
includes every word ever written. People often do not realize
that it is the Holy Spirit who is leading them to various writings. We feel
that we are following our own personal likes or dislikes. What we fail to
realize is that it is the Holy Spirit that gives us our attraction to certain
holy literature. I often ask a person what they have read and studied in
the last several years. It can give me a good indication of what the Holy
Spirit may be preparing them for, without their even realizing it.

The Holy Spirit has knowledge of every word we have ever read,
every word we are reading now, and every word we will ever read. How
many times have we thought a thought only to soon read the same ideas
written somewhere else as a confirmation? How many times has God
tried to warn us of something only to have that warning amplified and
repeated in something we have read? How many times have we read of a
particular circumstance only to realize later on that it was preparation for
something similar that soon would happen to us?

It is frightening, in a sense, when we realize how personally aware
the Holy Spirit is of each one of us, our unique situations in life, and
especially our hidden thoughts. If we come to realize how, through the

written word, God speaks to us in such a personal and intimate way, we would scarcely go a day without reading. In fact, we would continually search out God, his intimacy, wisdom, and love whenever we had a chance to open a book.

This is why it is a good idea for Anonymous Monks to always have a book at hand. We never know when God may give us the gift of a few moments to commune with him. Anonymous Monks try to carry a book at all times, whether in our cars, pockets, backpacks, or purses; whether we are on a business trip, vacation, taking a lunch break, or in the restroom. I am especially speaking of Sacred Scripture and spiritual books but I am not limiting the Holy Spirit who can use anything at anytime to speak to us, remembering that God once used a talking jackass to deliver a message to Balaam (Numbers 22:28).

Besides leading us and attracting us to a particular writing, the Holy Spirit also gives us the power to understand and comprehend what God is trying to say to us. So there is a twofold action. One, we are being guided to the literature and the other, our minds are being opened to the meaning of its contents. Both are the action of the Holy Spirit. We are simply the willing vessels, so to speak.

Through the written word the Holy Spirit encourages, teaches, exhorts, and corrects us as though we were the only person on earth. Reading is such an intimate and individual experience.

I will give you an example of how specifically the Holy Spirit can speak to us through the written word. This is sort of an embarrassing story to tell because it sounds a little far fetched, but since it is a good illustration of what I am trying to say I will share it.

Once, when one of my sons was about four years old, we were at a park near a deep stream. This can be dangerous in Florida, which is where we lived at the time, because of the threat of alligators. While we were at the park I met two women and quite spontaneously became engaged in an evangelical type of conversation, which included my sharing with them about the Lord. My son, meanwhile, was playing near the stream. The thought occurred to me that there could be alligators around but I continued to share with the woman anyway. (The thought occurred to me because just a few months earlier a three-year-old girl had been attacked by an alligator.)

The next day we went back to the park and a young park attendant mentioned to us that there had been an alligator spotted near the area where we had met the two women the day before. I was shocked.

That night while I was lying in bed a sudden terror came across my entire being. The thought of what could have happened to my son caused me great distress. This was especially frightful to me because I felt this particular son was unusually wise and holy for his age. Also, the thought of how my husband would have reacted if this son had been injured while I was talking to strangers about Jesus was equally frightful since he often spoke against the faith.

Suddenly, an overwhelming urge to go to my Bible overtook me. I could not resist the urge to get out of bed and pick up my Bible. Without consciously knowing why, I started to turn and scan the pages as if I knew where I was going. My fingers went to the Book of Job as if I had knowledge of the exact Scripture passage and its place. I stopped at chapter 40, verse 25, and read the passage. To my amazement, the passage I was pointing to emphasized God's power over the crocodile or leviathan (Job 41). Of course, joy spread throughout my whole being as I knelt before the Word of God, giving thanks. Like most people, I was not aware that crocodiles were even mentioned in the Bible.

This is an extraordinary example, but it well illustrates how real the Holy Spirit actually is. God is truly concerned about the daily events of our lives. After all, if the birds and God's creatures often know how to take care of themselves merely by instinct, is it so hard to believe that we humans could also understand our God almost by instinct?

It is very likely that as human beings we are often simply too distracted with doing our own will and too busy fulfilling our own desires to hear what the Holy Spirit is saying. By simplifying our lives and stopping throughout our day to listen as we read, we place ourselves in a position whereby the Holy Spirit can speak to us. This intimate communication between God and humankind is so exciting that any amount of self-sacrifice is worth it.

The Holy Spirit can also lead us through the Scriptures and teach us in-depth spiritual realities. It was through reading and extensive study of Sacred Scripture that I converted to Catholicism at the age of thirty-six. Through reading and studying I eventually came to realize that everything the Holy Spirit was sharing with me was being taught by the Catholic Church.

The Holy Spirit has the ability to teach us as though we had the very best scholar sitting right in front of us, but the Holy Spirit is better than a scholar because only he has the power to open our minds to the meaning of the Scriptures. Let us remember the words of Christ, "The Advocate, the Holy Spirit whom the Father will send in my name, will teach you everything, and remind you of all that I have said to you" (John 14:26). The Holy Spirit leads us to the writings that he wishes to use in order to communicate to us and enlighten us. By this enlightenment an average person can sometimes comprehend more about truth in a fraction of the time than if he had formally studied for years.

I am not condemning formal study. We all need to take responsibility for our relationship with God and our intellectual understanding of God by studying Sacred Scripture ourselves. By doing so, we will not be led astray by anyone who uses the name of Jesus and claims to know him (Ephesians 4:14). By study and reading we will all be able to give a strong and well-thought explanation of our faith when necessary (1 Peter 3:15).

As Anonymous Monks, we strive to devote a good amount of time each day to the practice of reading and study. It is a good idea to carry with us, either in our backpacks, pockets, purses, or cars, something spiritual to read at all times. We never know when the Lord will give us the gift of a few precious moments to communicate with him through the written word. (Writing or compiling documents, books, articles, and so on, should not replace the prayerful practice of spiritual reading and Scripture study.[1])

1. "Statute on Unity and Pluralism," 1969, *Trappist Guidelines*, #3.

🔊 Chapter 15 🔊
Taking a Break

Prayer should therefore be short and pure, unless
perhaps it is prolonged under the inspiration of divine grace.
RULE OF ST. BENEDICT, 20:4.

🔊A s Anonymous Monks we strive to remain at peace at all
times. This means that we should try to plan small amounts
of time each day to recollect ourselves in order to regain our composure.
Periods of solitude are usually necessary for us to experience a deeper
sense of God's peace.

Even if we break for only five-minute intervals we will be able to
calm ourselves down spiritually, mentally, and physically by taking
breaks alone throughout our day. During this time we can examine our
conscience and reflect on God. [1] Taking a break can mean stepping into
the restroom, going to the water cooler, or sitting out on the back porch,
a spare room, or some other place where we can be alone with God. The
amount of solitude that each one of us needs each day can greatly vary
from person to person.

While at my place of employment, I used to take my breaks out in
my car where I could sit in the sun and think. My father used to just go
for a walk by himself or sit in another room for a few moments. As a stay-
at-home mom, I used to run out and get a newspaper as soon as my
husband came home from work just to recollect myself. (At the time we
had small children so I had to plan the best I could for a small break.)
Sometimes, I would have to ask my husband to watch the children while
I went into the bathroom to get away. Of course, as many mothers and
fathers do, I tried to plan the children's naps at the same time so that I
had an hour or two to myself. Sometimes, the only time I had alone was

when I used the bathroom or took a shower, and even then being alone was not always possible. So, as you can see, I was constantly trying to make little plans in anticipation of some time alone with God.

Jogging, weight lifting, swimming, golf, and other sports that are usually performed alone can become a wonderful time for meditation, as well as a great opportunity for reflection, that is, if we can participate in these activities in a relaxed manner.

We should try not to force breaks when there seems to be no opportunity. Nagging or complaining to get a break is not really the best scenario either. Being too concerned about getting a break can sometimes cause us to be more unrecollected than if we just did without one.

If we have tried to work out a break time the best we can but things still do not work out, perhaps we should accept that God knows how much time we can take. Maybe we are stronger than we think. God will give us a break when he sees fit, and when he does we will become even more grateful because we will have a real awareness that the moments of solitude and rest were God's gift to us.

Let us also remember that if for some reason, as often happens to many of us, we do lose our cool or even fall apart at the seams, we can remember the old Alcoholics Anonymous adage "one day at a time," or even perhaps "one minute at a time." If we get into an argument with someone, we try to stop and reflect the best we can by praying for ourselves and those involved. If possible, we try to make up with the person or persons immediately, hopefully before the sun goes down. It is often said, it is not good to go to bed angry. Let us try to break throughout our day in order to catch ourselves in the event that we might depart from the love of God and love for others.

There was also an adage I learned from Alanon (friends of alcoholics). It was the acronym H.A.L.T. It stood for "hungry, angry, lonely, tired." This means that if we are really struggling through our day it may very well be one of these things we need to address. Often a small meal is a practical way for us to recollect ourselves in Christ. If we are angry we can speak to a friend and share our burdens so that we may resume our mindfulness of Christ. If we feel lonely, even lonely from too much time in prayer, we can take a break and meet with others to regain our balance. Even monks that are hermits come out once in a while to get in touch. If we are tired we can take whatever opportunities God gives us for rest. This is what is known as self-knowledge. By being more aware of why we are getting anxious and disturbed in spirit, mind, and body, through practice we will be able to catch ourselves before we lose our peace completely by acting out our frustrations.

Some other helps for allowing us to deepen our sense of solitude are praying in the dark, wearing a hood or a hat, temporarily turning off the radio or television, taking a break from crowded places, and occasionally limiting time spent on the telephone. I sometimes turn the ringer off on the phone and allow the answering machine to pick up calls for a short time. We might also temporarily move the phone to another room where we can't hear it ringing.

If we live in a noisy area, it may help to wear earplugs in order to obtain the real silence that can foster a deeper sense of solitude. Once I went to the drag races with my family and, like many others, I purchased some earplugs. To my amazement, I had a deep sense of solitude as I walked throughout the crowded and very noisy park. It occurred to me how effective earplugs could be for those of us who dwell in busy traffic areas, construction areas, or crowded living facilities. Earplugs are also a great way to avoid the sound of lawn mowers, chain saws, loud parties next door, and so on. (If you choose to wear earplugs, just be careful not to place yourselves, your children, or others in any danger while wearing them.)

1. "Statute on Unity and Pluralism," 1969, *Trappist Guidelines*, #6.

Chapter 16

Keeping Possessions from Possessing You

"All things should be common possession of all," as it is written, "so that no one presumes to call anything his own" (Acts 4:32).
RULE OF ST. BENEDICT, 33:6.

What are health, riches, and freedom, if they go against growth toward God? Can a person who has money who is not growing toward God, the source of all life, truly be considered rich? Can a person whose wounds have been healed, who is not growing deeper in Christ, really be considered healthy? Can a person who can do what he or she wants but is not growing closer to God, really be considered free?

The answer to these questions is "no." If a person who is impoverished is drawing closer to God in the midst of poverty, isn't he or she really wealthy? If a person grows into deeper communion with Christ because of his or her disease, isn't that person really growing in health? If someone is seeking God in the universe within their own heart and mind but happens to be locked in a cell, isn't that person not really free?

So, an Anonymous Monk need not be concerned with others' narrow-minded perspective of health, wealth, and freedom, but should be concerned whether he is growing in God instead.

Remember, God is eternal, and we will grow deeper in him forever. Anyone who thinks like this is already in heaven. There is no fear of death or disease or anything else because "perfect love casts out fear" (1 John 4:18). Nothing can separate us from the love of God (Romans 8:35–39).

Remember how many of the saints would speak of their calling as beginning in the next life. So, as Anonymous Monks we need only to be concerned with growing in God, and we shall be drawn into eternal life with him.

Without drawing any undue attention to ourselves, we should try to live as simply as possible in reference to clothing, cars, housing, and the like. Simplicity does not mean that we do not buy quality items that we need. It means that we try to break the consumerist habit of "keeping up with the Joneses" and simply buy what we truly need according to our situation in life. Like many other practices mentioned in this book, simplicity is an attitude that must be developed over time. [1]

Of course, if you are a banker or have some other position that requires more sophisticated attire, you will be required to have a wardrobe that is respectable. Again, that does not mean that we have *carte blanche* to go overboard. If we are wealthy and do not understand simplicity, we should focus on cultivating a simplicity of heart if not an outward simplicity. (Those who are poor and imprisoned should try to see the value of their forced simplicity and continue to do all that they can to at least obtain the basics in life.) Anonymous Monks should avoid frivolous shopping trips to malls and stores.

When purchasing items it is a good idea to make a list of what we actually need and stick to it, not adding things to our order out of impulse. Again, it's prudent to pay by cash or check and rarely by credit. Frugality used to be the norm, but today when most of us have more than enough, it almost has to be taught.

Anonymous Monks try to live a frugal lifestyle. In other words, we try to be extra careful not to be wasteful. When we have to shop for anything we should try to get the best price possible, unless getting the best price actually costs more because of driving farther and spending more on gas.

Anonymous Monks try to save leftover food and have it as a snack or use it again in another recipe instead of throwing it away. We also consider using coupons whenever possible. If we need clothes for some special event, something that we may only wear once, we consider borrowing an outfit from a friend. Borrowing things from others can be a great act of humility, as long as it's not overdone. If we cannot borrow the items needed, we might even try a thrift shop or discount department store.

We can often find uses for old items that we might otherwise throw away. However, I am not condoning our becoming packrats—it is certainly okay to throw something away, if need be. Let's not throw out items belonging to others unless we ask them first. And, if we do discard something, let's try to do so in the most perfect way possible, such as recycling newspapers, glass bottles, aluminum cans, and the like.

Frugality may be extended to the prudent use of natural resources, such as water, wood products, and especially nonrenewable resources such as the multitude of oil-based products. The electricity shortage in some parts of the country reminds us that electricity is not wasted without serious social, and economic repercussions. Conservation is the easiest and most effective way of preserving the earth's precious resources for future generations. Anonymous Monks in loving service of our neighbor include the generation to come after us in our thoughts and actions. My frugality today may assure their basic survival tomorrow.

Frugality means that it's best to buy items out of necessity, obligation, or under obedience, such as purchasing a particular item because a spouse or employer has requested it. Still, even when we are asked, if the items aren't really necessary, we should try to talk about it with the intention of dissuading the purchase, if possible. (For some people, due to a lack of spending control, it may be a good idea to avoid malls as much as possible.)

Because of the anxiety associated with owing money, especially large sums, frugal Anonymous Monks can organize their budget in such a way as to work toward becoming completely debt free. The use of credit cards could be limited and used only under absolute necessity, or under obedience. Remember the Scripture passages, "the borrower is the slave of the lender" (Proverbs 22:7) and "owe no one anything, except to love one another" (Romans 13:8). Some of us may be in circumstances that require the assistance of a financial advisor. Many of us have friends and family who are excellent business people who could offer sound advice.

We can acquire so many things that tending to our possessions can become cumbersome and complicate our lives unnecessarily, draining us of energy that we could offer to God in prayer. Developing a lifestyle of simplicity systematically eliminates the external clutter that, over time, has infiltrated our minds and hearts. Simplicity of our life aids simplicity of mind so that we can focus on the present moment and not on the diversions that can come from owning an inordinate amount of possessions.

Through simplicity, we reopen our senses, the channels to our souls, so that we can begin to see God in all things and, perhaps, even think more clearly and creatively. Simplicity does not mean that we are simple-minded or stupid, far from it. When we are intentionally living simple lives, it is a sign of self-mastery and self-control (Galatians 5:22–23).

Not only can we live frugally and simply by way of our possessions, we can also live simply in a very important part of our lives, which is how we relate to others. We used to say in Alanon, "Carry the message, not the person," which means that we can encourage others without having to get immersed in all the details of their lives and troubles. Getting overly involved in others' personal dilemmas can cause us to take on unnecessary burdens—physically, emotionally, and mentally. We also used to say in Alanon, "Detach with love," meaning that we love the person not the sin.

Having simplicity in relationships means that we are active rather than reactive. This means that we take time to listen and to think before responding. When we quit reacting by remaining in control of our thoughts and actions, we experience the peace that comes with being a mature person. Just because others may be stirring up a whirlwind of trouble, we need not get entangled; we need not try to save them from all of their troubles.

Detaching from others is especially important when it comes to listening to gossip and slander. Listening to people maliciously put down others and allowing ourselves to get involved in destructive conversations by taking sides can cause us great distraction when it comes time to pray. Often, the best thing that we can do for others is simply to love them and pray for them. This is why even in our efforts to evangelize it is often better not to get caught up in deep theological arguments with our neighbors, friends, family, and associates. You may win the debate but you may also cause unnecessary hardship, stress, and bad feelings.

L ove is a simple and sincere language that everyone can understand. This is why Paul said, "We have behaved in the world with frankness and godly sincerity, not by earthly wisdom but by the grace of God—and all the more toward you" (2 Corinthians 1:12).

One major point in regard to simplicity is that sin complicates our lives. Holy living simplifies our hearts and minds. Sin causes us to feel frustrated and confused because we soon find out that when we sin, we lose our peace of mind and our ability to pray is hindered. There is no sin that is worth disrupting our precious gift of prayer. Sometimes, when a person is extremely rude to me or others, one of my first thoughts is "Does this person pray?"—probably not. No one can be rude to someone and then sit peacefully in the presence of God. This is why Jesus said, "So when you are offering your gift at the altar, if you remember that your brother or sister has something against you, leave your gift there before the altar and go; first be reconciled to your brother or sister, and then come and offer your gift" (Matthew 5:23–24).

Obtaining simplicity in relationships may include making amends and apologizing for our part in any division. Even if we are not to blame, we can at least apologize for having offended others. It seems like work, and it is, but the freedom to love and to pray is worth any sacrifices that we have to make. All sacrifices seem like nothing compared to the presence of God in our lives. Paul says, "We also boast in our sufferings, knowing that suffering produces endurance, and endurance produces character, and character produces hope, and hope does not disappoint us, because God's love has been poured into our hearts through the Holy Spirit that has been given to us" (Romans 5:3–5).

As I have mentioned throughout this book, when we do everything out of love for God it becomes prayer. This is our goal and aim as Anonymous Monks.

1. "Statute on Unity and Pluralism," 1969, *Trappist Guidelines*, #11.

Chapter 17

Overdoing Good Deeds

These people "fear the Lord," and do not become elated
over their good deeds; they judge it is the Lord's power,
not their own, that brings about good in them.

RULE OF ST. BENEDICT, PROLOGUE: 29.

As persons who are called to a deep prayer life, it can be a temptation for us to stay busy. Staying busy can become a way of avoiding being alone with God, especially if God is calling us to that aloneness. Being alone with God can be difficult, because not only do we have to face him, but we also have to face ourselves.

As Anonymous Monks, our primary way of serving others and the world is through prayer. We are called to spend "quality time" alone with God in prayer. The word "monk" comes from a Greek word meaning "one," "single," or "alone" with God.

We may find ourselves called to perform extra work activities. In helping to discern our motives for any activity, let us examine our intentions. An important intention for any activity, including prayer, should be our own salvation. "Work out your salvation with fear and trembling" (Philippians 2:12), my point being that we can lead others only as far as we are willing to go ourselves.

When discerning whether or not we should take on extra activity that goes beyond our normal day-to-day obligations, we can ask ourselves some questions that may help us to clarify our intentions and discern what it is that the Lord is expecting of us.

First, let us ask, is the activity drawing us closer to God or is it distracting and diverting us from God? In my state in life, am I required or obliged to take up this work? Would others think less of me if I didn't do this work? Am I obliged as a housewife, doctor, teacher, mother, son, etc., to commit myself to this activity?

In order to get another viewpoint, I could ask those around me, especially those with whom I live or have close personal ties, what they think of this work. Often, those close to us are the best at seeing things more clearly. (I suggest using this type of discernment even in regard to religious activities, such as volunteer work at church.)

If we are not obliged to get actively involved, perhaps God is calling us to get involved in other ways, such as by prayer or financial support. In some cases, it may not be the activity itself but the way we are doing it that is causing us to feel distanced from God. Perhaps, it is the right thing, but the wrong time. Or, perhaps, we are taking it too seriously by taking on too much at once.

In some instances, we may feel called to be involved simply by staying home and spending more time in our domestic "cloister." Let us not forget the value of physical separation from the world and our strong belief in the power of prayer to save, heal, and restore.

When performing charitable acts, we must be on guard not to do for others what they should be doing for themselves. I used to continually watch neighborhood children in my home. Some of the mothers and fathers really needed my help while others were going to the beach and shirking their responsibilities. In this circumstance, performing an inordinate amount of good deeds could be considered as my needlessly interfering in the responsible lives of others. I have read that a Buddhist master once said that sometimes compassion was something that needed to be overcome.

It can be a temptation for prayerful people to feel compelled to keep moving, to keep doing, especially, when it is time for prayer. This compulsion has been called the "messiah complex," meaning that a person feels that he or she must actively save the world almost single-handedly. It could also be pride, in the sense of always needing to be seen doing some good work.

In regard to hospitality, let us try to receive guests in an ordered, graceful way. If we plan our time wisely, we can often reduce the temptation to become frantic. When it comes to major ongoing commitments, Anonymous Monks should use prudence and perhaps even seek the advice of a spiritual director or someone we count as wise, especially if these are commitments that may severely impede our vocation to prayer.

Let us remember how Mary of Bethany sat at the feet of Jesus, giving him all her attention in love, and Jesus responded by saying, "There is need of only one thing. Mary has chosen the better part, which will not be taken away from her" (Luke 10:42).

"One thing" means that in all that we do we should be going deeper into Christ. If God is calling us to a particular work we should be able to focus on loving him and others without getting caught up in a whirlwind of tasks that can cause us to lose peace. Some people can be involved in many activities and still remain loving and kind, all the while focusing on Christ. For them it is not a distraction.

Others who are called to a more hidden life can be very distracted from Christ, the path of true love, even in seemingly pious acts. This varies greatly from person to person. And it is one of the reasons why it is so important to have a good spiritual director or companion who can help us discern what is best.

🌿 Chapter 18 🌿
Making Your Speech
a Prayer

*"Who will dwell in your tent, Lord; who will find rest
upon your Holy Mountain?" (Psalms 14[15]:1) . . .
One who walks without blemish and is just in all his dealings;
who speaks the truth from his heart and has not practiced deceit
with his tongue; who has not wronged a fellow man in anyway,
nor listened to slanders against his neighbor."*

RULE OF ST. BENEDICT, PROLOGUE: 23, 25.

S o that the punishment for sin may be avoided," [1] let us use care when choosing to speak. God has knowledge of every word that we have ever spoken. We could all probably spend the rest of our lifetime just making up for all of our bad choices in speech. Many of us would probably do well to speak as little as possible from here on out. I had a grandfather who rarely spoke and didn't appear to be unusually wise or religious, but at least he seemed to possess enough wisdom to speak infrequently.

Saint Benedict says in his rule, "The ninth step of humility is that a monk remains silent, not speaking unless asked a question" (p. 37). This is a very important statement if we really wish to follow God's will in our speech. As was mentioned in the previous chapter, the best intention for performing any action might be necessity, obedience (doing the will of another), or obligation.

This also holds true with our speech. If we only speak when we are spoken to we can be attentive to the will of God in our speech because we are speaking under obedience to the other person. This is also true when I must speak to others because of my occupation, and of course when I speak to my friends and family members in a helpful, respectful, and friendly manner.

I am not saying that we should strictly adhere to the precept of only speaking when spoken to. I am just offering a reflection as to why Saint Benedict may have said these things. What I am suggesting is that we, as Anonymous Monks, place the emphasis on the quality of our speech as opposed to the quantity.

Sometimes, in order not to appear aloof, we must speak for the sake of being friendly or charitable, and of welcoming others as Christ. In some cases, we can appear to be rude or unnecessarily distancing ourselves from others if we don't speak. So, you see, we must always be aware of charity toward all, not because we do not respect silence, but because we do not want to offend others by doing something of which they have little or no understanding. I am speaking of our devotion toward silence. We try to deal with people according to their weakness and not according to the areas in which we are knowledgeable (1 Corinthians 10:28–29).

Let us also remember that words are extremely powerful. God created the entire world and everything in it with words. Remember how God "said," let there be light, and light came into being. Similarly, our words have the power to bring life or death.

When we speak, let us carefully put a guard over our mouths. Let us try to speak only when we really have something that needs saying. [2] When we do choose to speak, let our words be words that encourage and bring life, instead of words that humiliate and bring death.

There are many times that we all struggle throughout our day. We certainly do not want to add to another's burden by saying something that is sarcastic or rude. Remember that the root meaning of the word "sarcasm" actually means to "tear the flesh."

If we feel ourselves becoming agitated, let us pray silently to allow ourselves time to calm down, so that we will not say, or do, something we will regret later. If, as is likely, we do say something that we regret, let us quickly apologize to the persons involved and try to do something special for them in order to make amends.

Also, it will help us to confess to another the things that we have said that we shouldn't have said. This practice will help us to take responsibility for our actions and avoid the same mistake in the future. Do not be concerned about presenting yourself as someone who never falls. Do not let pride keep you from growing in virtue.

As long as we continue admitting to God and to others that we have made bad choices, we will be on the road to breaking our bad habits and growing more and more in the likeness of Christ. Remember that when we speak it should be the Holy Spirit who is actually doing the speaking (see Mark 13:11).

W hen we talk to one another we can try to do so with the love of a mother, brother, or sister. If we are at the store or at work or when we drive, we can be courteous, seeing others not as someone we do not know or someone who has no relevance in our life but as someone who is truly our mother, brother, or father.

Let even our body language convey gentleness and concern for all. Let us be viewed by others as peacemakers in the way that we present ourselves and in our speech. Our actions should speak louder than our words. Let even the tone and volume of our speech convey warmth and love to all. This may seem a little unrealistic, especially for those who have to deal with children and adolescents on a regular basis. If we do raise our voice, let it be in such a way that the person knows that we love them, that it is what they are doing that we do not approve.

Children deserve the same respect and in some ways even more respect than adults. Usually the child being yelled at has not committed nearly as many sins as the adult who is chastising them. Also, remember that God will judge us as strictly as we judge others. If we insist on perfection from children or anyone else, God will hold our feet to the fire as well. With the same measure that we consider others will it be measured back to us.

Those who cannot speak because of illness can come to know the value of silence. They can offer up this silence in order to make up for all the times when people speak words that they should not. This reparation is a powerful work, considering that sins of speech are probably one of the most abundant and prevalent types of sin.

Let us also try to avoid talking excessively over the telephone. I do not refer to those who make their living on the phone. I mean refraining from talking on and on, entangled in frivolous conversation and small talk. If we write to someone instead of telephoning, we naturally choose our words more carefully. It is wise not to let too much time pass before contacting persons who might be hurt if we don't at least write occasionally. [3] We can at least send holiday and birthday cards if we are able. Obviously, Anonymous Monks strive not to gossip, slander, or speak maliciously.

We can, with subtlety, let others know that we see each person in the best light and do not make any judgments. A good rule of thumb is the trusty old adage, "If you don't have anything good to say, don't say anything." Christ came to be the Savior of the world, not its judge.

It can also help to make the sign of the cross whenever our minds and hearts begin to drift from God. Making the sign of the cross frequently throughout our day is a good reminder that the Holy Trinity is with us always. Making the sign of the cross will give us strength when we are tempted to do and say the wrong things.

When we have conversations concerning a sensitive or confidential matter, we must be careful not to mention the matter to anyone, unless it is required by us because of our position in life. For example, if I hear from a troubled person in the community that he may harm himself or others, I may have to report this to my superior, employer, wife, husband, doctor, etc. If I am a father and my son tells me something that his mother should know, using prudence, I have to share it. Again, because of my position in life, I may be required to divulge certain information.

Anonymous Monks try not to be silent to the point that they give others the impression that they are purposely not speaking to them. We do not want to appear objectionally or unusually quiet. The key to this spiritual practice and to our spirituality in general is to do what can be done without drawing undue attention to ourselves.

We should avoid the temptation of purposely not speaking to someone because of hard feelings. If we do get into a quarrel with someone, let us be careful not to let the sun go down without making up. Preferably, only a few minutes should pass before reconciling.

Let me tell you a little story to help explain the importance of reconciliation. A mother and son once got into a quarrel. The mother told the son that he was worthless and a hindrance to the family. That night the boy decided to run away from home and was accidentally killed as he did so. The mother had to live for the rest of her life with that last horrible thing that she said to her son. We or anyone else we quarrel with could die at any time. It is best to interact with others, in word and deed, as though it were our last day of life.

1. *Rule of St. Benedict*, ch. 6.
2. John Climacus: *Ladder of Divine Ascent*, p. 158.
3. John Climacus: *Ladder of Divine Ascent*, p. 112.

🐚 Chapter 19 🐚

Making Your Eating a Prayer

"Renounce yourself in order to follow Christ"
(Matthew 16:24; Luke 9:23); . . .
do not pamper yourself, but love fasting.
RULE OF ST. BENEDICT, 4:10.

It is highly advisable to get the permission of your spiritual director, your spouse, and your physician before beginning any type of fasting. Fasting without the approval and knowledge of others can be a sign of pride, because we can be acting on feelings of competing to see who is holiest by who is fasting the most. All fasting should be done thoughtfully and with permission. We have a strong warning in the following quote from the rule of Saint Benedict: "Everyone should, however, make known to the abbot what he intends to do, since it ought to be done with his prayer and approval. Whatever is undertaken without permission of the spiritual father will be reckoned as presumption and vainglory, not deserving a reward. Therefore, everything must be done with the abbot's approval."

Fasting is a form of self-inflicted redemptive suffering. Besides uniting us to the poor and infirm who are often forced to fast, abstaining from certain foods that we eat habitually can liberate our minds and bodies. It refocuses energies normally devoted to enjoying and obtaining our favorite types of food and drink. This extra brain energy can give us more clarity in our thinking about the things of God, about what direction God would have us go.

This is why persons in the Bible like Jesus and Moses and the Israelites fasted in the desert. In the desert there is nothing but ourselves and God—and perhaps confrontations with various demons (temptations)—to challenge us. The aloneness and separateness that is created from certain foods becomes our own little desert where we are free and ready to hear from God in our need.

Our desire for certain foods turns our attention to desire for God because we become more aware that we need his strength. This clears the way for healing to take place in our selves at all levels. By fasting we can also bring healing to others all over the world. When speaking of a type of demon from whom the apostles could not rid a young boy, Jesus said, "This kind can only come out through prayer" (Mark 9:29).

Out of love and reverence for God, we seek to make every activity a prayer, including eating and drinking. Below are a few helpful suggestions for helping us to stay mindful of God and to unite ourselves to the poor while we eat.

Anonymous Monks, in keeping with the monastic tradition of the desert monks, could try to avoid eating meat. [1] Meat is expensive and there are many people all over the world who simply cannot afford it. So we can make our eating a prayer by secretly and purposely bringing an element of God into our eating by avoiding some foods and eating other foods out of charity.

For example, there may be times when it may be best to eat meat in order not to draw any undue attention to ourselves such as when meat is being served to us by a host and everyone else is eating meat. It could seem prideful and needlessly offensive if we were to suddenly announce that we do not eat meat or this or that. In this case we should gratefully and obediently eat whatever is placed before us, not asking for extra condiments or anything else, but expressing an attitude of thanks to God and to those who serve us. [2]

Anonymous Monks, when cooking for themselves, can try to prepare plain and simple meals without spices. In time, we will appreciate the natural taste of foods and be grateful for them just as they are.

We eat simply to make ourselves ever mindful that we live for God alone, and he is the source of our true joy, not food, or anything else. I am not saying that we should not enjoy our food and be grateful. I am saying that we should not live for the joy of eating. We will be ever mindful of God's providence in providing us with food by thanking him in prayer before we eat and not complaining about what he has provided.

Those who are chronically ill and can eat little or nothing should see their abstinence as a gift from God. Of course, we may make use of all the medical help that is available to remedy illness, but when all is said and done, we should accept our abstinence as a gift from God that comes with its own graces. It is wise for everyone to get their physician's opinion and approval about abstaining from meat. The sick and infirm should eat meat and anything else that their doctor deems necessary. [3]

Some persons, especially women, can become anemic from not getting enough iron—they need to eat meat to maintain good health. I was told by my physician to eat a certain type of salt because of a thyroid condition. We should be good stewards of our health and even have our blood checked occasionally to make sure that we are not deficient because of our fasting.

Anonymous Monks would do well to avoid eating or drinking anything that contains caffeine or alcohol. We would also do well to avoid the use of all tobacco products. These items can be highly addictive and can almost become a god to those persons who apparently cannot live without them. To some people, however, these things are merely minor luxuries. If you simply cannot give them up, try to use them in moderation and avoid abusing the good health that God has given you. If we drink alcohol to the degree that either we ourselves or others feel that it is affecting our life adversely, then we should humbly seek help at a qualified alcohol treatment center.

1. "Statute on Unity and Pluralism," 1969, *Trappist Guidelines*, #9.
2. John Climacus: *Ladder of Divine Ascent*, p. 161.
3. *Rule of St. Benedict*, ch. 36.

ᐓ Chapter 20 ᐕ
Using the Media Prayerfully

Listen readily to holy reading,
and devote yourself often to prayer.
RULE OF ST. BENEDICT, 4:55–56.

Anonymous Monks will use extreme prudence when watching secular television, listening to secular radio, using the Internet, and reading newspapers, magazines, and the like. [1] It is good to put a guard over our eyes and ears by shunning even the appearance of evil. We may be kidding ourselves if we think that these things cannot harm us.

Any viewing or listening to programming that is of a perverted or violent nature is to be avoided. We can learn to change the channel as soon as we sense that these things are about to appear or be heard. The devil is a braggart and loves to rouse our curiosity about what he is doing, especially when it is time for us to pray. Besides, it is only human nature that, when we go to pray, what we have seen and heard in the last several hours will surface in our memories.

By watching something questionable we could severely affect the peace of mind necessary for imageless prayer. I am speaking of the type of prayer whereby we simply rest in God's love without pictures of anything in our mind's eye or thoughts concerning anything. If negative things do come to mind during prayer, we can include these things in our prayer by giving them over to God, but it is better not to expose ourselves to a barrage of evil.

Apparently, many movie producers feel that violence is entertaining. However, we must be violently concerned about the proper use of violence in ridding ourselves of sin. Jesus showed us the proper use of violence when he whipped the money changers who had reduced the temple to a place of commerce (John 2:13–17). We should violently rid our own temples, our own bodies of the excessive concern for material things, so that we can turn our temple into a house of prayer. Let's not be allured by the promise of many good things that the media falsely offers.

It would be wise to limit our television viewing to a reasonable amount of time each day. Anything more than two hours a day may be excessive. This figure obviously does not include those who may have to watch television or use communications media for a living. (Of course, in the case of an emergency, such as a hurricane, we do need to keep informed about what is going on.)

1. "Statute on Unity and Pluralism," 1969, *Trappist Guidelines*, #7.

☜ Chapter 21 ☞
Our Home
Is in Our Heart

The workshop where we are to toil faithfully at all tasks
is the enclosure and stability of the community.
RULE OF ST. BENEDICT, 4:78.

☜S tability" means that we are committed to a place and to the people who inhabit that place. It could mean those in our own homes, those who live on our street, and those with whom we work. It means that we are committed to our family, to our city, state, and country, etc. Ideally, it would be nice if we, as Anonymous Monks, could commit to one area until death, as an anchor of prayer for that place. In this place we believe that we will find all that we will ever need to journey back to God (Abbot Francis Kline).

However, living in the modern world, stability for some may not mean never changing places or never coming into contact with new people. It may simply mean developing in ourselves the awareness that God has brought us amongst certain people at a particular time for a particular reason, even if only for the moment.

No matter our degree of physical stability, let us love those around us with a firm spiritual stability. (A person can be physically living in one area while his or her heart and mind are far off in another area). We can see everyone we meet as someone whom God has called us to assist on their journey back to him, even if it means only to pray for them and nothing else.

If we are placed with mean and disagreeable people, it may be because God knows that we are the only persons who would be willing to pray for them. Even then, our love is stable. God often lets people agitate us, so that we are forced to pray for them if we wish to remain in his peace. God knows that they are really in need of our prayers and that we may very well be the only persons on earth who are willing to do so.

Loving everyone equally clears the path for Jesus to pray inside of us. We cannot fool ourselves into thinking that we do not have to love all equally. We can only love God as much as we love the person that we love the least. In the Our Father we pray, "Thy kingdom come, thy will be done, on earth as it is in heaven." In heaven God, like a good and perfect father, loves all of his children equally. We must also strive to love all equally if we are going to be vessels used to bring God's Kingdom to earth, remembering that charity always begins at home.

In reference to equality, even though some of us are fathers, mothers, and priests (who are also referred to as Father), we may wish to remember Jesus saying, " 'Who is my mother, and who are my brothers?' And pointing to his disciples, he said, '"Here are my mother and my brothers! For whoever does the will of my Father in heaven is my brother and sister and mother'" (Matthew 12:48–50).

I am saying this because we can love someone as a type of fatherly figure in the sense that this person is a mentor, but we have to be careful not to aggrandize anyone with an exaggerated patronage or reverence. By doing so we could become divisive in our thinking and possibly even prejudicial toward those who may not quite measure up to the good example of ourselves or of others.

Ultimately, "There is only one who is good" (Matthew 19:17). "But you are not to be called rabbi, for you have one teacher, and you are all students. And call no one your father on earth, for you have one Father—the one in heaven" (Matthew 23:8). I am saying all of this in order to help us to truly see every human being as equal.

If we do not see everyone as equal, or if we have inordinate attachments to some people, this clinging to persons as opposed to God can keep us from fulfilling God's highest good in our lives because we can be, in a sense, loving those persons more than God. "Whoever loves father or mother more than me is not worthy of me, and whoever loves son or daughter more than me is not worthy of me" (Matthew 10:37). It will help us tremendously with our commitment to our families and the whole world if we truly think of everyone, even our spouses, children, and parents, as our brother and sister with God as our heavenly Father.

We must be especially on guard for any serious division that could threaten our physical or spiritual stability. Our stability assures us our security. Having security means that we are stable in our living situations. This frees our minds to be involved in prayer and the eternal things of God. Remember that Moses, as negative as the Israelites were toward him, led them to the Promised Land. Moses continued to intercede to God on their behalf, never abandoning the Israelites, never divorcing them, and God never divorces us.

Let us also remember that, even though the Israelites were very difficult to deal with at times, God seriously chastised Moses for his impatience with them at the rock of Meribah (Numbers 20:12). God wants all to come to him and takes our calling to bring others to him very seriously. If God punished the holy Moses for his slight impatience, what loss may we suffer for our grave intolerance and impatience?

S erious division such as divorce can severely hinder our prayer life. The radical rupture in our lives, not just materially but spiritually, with our spouses caused by divorce can greatly hinder our ability to stay fixed on God. This is because God is love. And "love is patient; love is kind . . ." (1 Corinthians 13:4). Anonymous Monks can never divorce anyone in their heart and still maintain union with God. If, by some tragedy, we are civilly and legally divorced, we try to be ever so careful not to turn a cold heart toward our former spouse.

I knew of a young woman who came into quite a bit of money from a court settlement. Having had marital problems and now being financially stable she wished to be rid of her husband. Her family encouraged her. One day she wrote a scathing letter to her soon-to-be ex-husband. On the way back from delivering the note she got in a horrible automobile accident. While she was dying in the hospital she called for her husband to come to her side. She died. She was only about twenty-six years old.

I do not know if her husband made it to the hospital, but, as you can see, her attitude radically changed when she knew that she was dying. Remembrance of death is a gift and a grace. It will help us to be ever mindful of the importance of our commitment to all those around us and realize, like Moses, that time is short and we must stay committed to each other as we struggle to get to the Promised Land. Doing so will give us the best kind of stability, that is, the stability of our undying and unconditional love.

Part of our stability can also include enclosure. "Enclosure" means that we keep our moving about throughout our day to a minimum, for the sake of focusing our attention on God. Enclosure can also mean that we keep our traveling to a minimum, except when we are called away because of obligation, necessity, or obedience.

Many of us have considered changing professions, places of employment, or locations, in favor of those more suitable for a prayerful monastic life. Many persons have left high-paying jobs in search of the peace that comes with simplicity and stability. This decision has to be discerned carefully, however. We should never make a major decision like leaving our job without prayerfully seeking the advice of others whom we count as wise. We should also get the opinions of those who would be affected by such a change.

To safeguard enclosure, and through the providence of God, someone close to the Anonymous Monk may be willing to help out by doing the shopping and running errands. [1,2]

Those of us who are imprisoned and chronically ill should be thankful and especially committed to the place where we live and the people that God has placed around us at this time. Let the prison, the sick ward, and wherever we happen to find ourselves, be our mission field.

1. "Statute on Unity and Pluralism," 1969, *Trappist Guidelines*, #7.
2. *Rule of St. Benedict*, 66:7.

Chapter 22

Attentiveness and Discipline

When [we] must punish them, [we] should use prudence
and avoid extremes; otherwise, by rubbing too hard
to remove the rust, [we] may break the vessel.

RULE OF ST. BENEDICT, 64:12.

A nonymous Monks who are raising children strive to refrain from yelling, name calling, and using rude tones of voice. God is, after all, a God of peace. We should refrain from telling anyone to shut up. No one should ever spank a child, unless he or she has complete self-control, not rushing in anger or flailing rage to punish the child, but speaking calmly to the child and explaining the problem and the punishment.

Some persons, especially those of us who were raised in violent homes, should avoid hitting anyone at any time.[1] God is a creative God, and he can provide us with creative ways of communicating.

Cleaning assignments are a great form of punishment. It can help a person burn off excess energy. It can also make a person feel really satisfied by seeing the work that has been accomplished. It may be helpful to supply the child being punished with his own gloves and bucket, or, if it meets the purpose, spray bottles filled with water or diluted cleaning solution. (Be sure to use cleaning liquids that are nontoxic.)

The child can spend a half-hour or so cleaning windows, counter-tops, practically everything in the house. Cleaning and vacuuming the car, mowing the lawn if they are old enough, cooking easy recipes, rearranging their bedrooms, cleaning out their desk drawers, or setting the dinner table are all positive ways of disciplining that accomplish something practically or esthetically.

Even though Scripture says, "Those who spare the rod hate their children" (Proverbs 13:24), hitting anyone can seriously disrupt the mindfulness of God necessary for prayerful monastic living. Many persons are simply unable to spank without going too far. Spanking that is hard enough to leave a bruise is too hard. Children over the age of eleven should receive some punishment other than spanking. Besides cleaning, older children could pay a fine, lose their allowance, or have extra chores. Perhaps they could be given a list of items to find on their own when the parents go grocery shopping.

Talk with older children, especially young adults, and explain that there are consequences to bad choices. Speak with them and even ask them what they think would be a good punishment under the circumstances. I once heard a Protestant preacher by the name of Marilyn Hickey say, "Rules without relationship lead to rebellion."

Disciplining, although negative in itself, is meant to have a positive result that leaves everyone involved closer and at peace. Correction is not intended to humiliate another. If we have gone too far in that direction, we quickly apologize and admit our sin with the intention of being more careful next time. If we wrong someone by going overboard in our actions and words, we need to make amends and perhaps do something extra special for them, by way of reparation.

If you are physically, mentally, or verbally hurting those around you on a regular basis, you probably need professional help. Talk openly about your problem to a qualified therapist. Take medication if necessary. Such therapy is nothing to be ashamed of. Many persons have mood disorders and have been successfully treated. It is not necessary or worth losing your family over a treatable emotional disorder. These disorders do not imply moral guilt and are sometimes the result of one's own imperfect upbringing. The chain of anger and violence must be broken at one of its links or it will go on forever.

This would also be a good time to talk about attentiveness toward others. When our children need us let's remember the words of Father Basil Pennington. When one of his spiritual sons asked him if he were too busy to speak to him, this most open and kindly abbot said, "I refuse to be busy." This is an excellent example of how we should talk to others, especially our children. If we are busy we can politely say that we would love to discuss this or that but that it would be better to do so at such and such a time.

Remember in the *Rule of St. Benedict* where it is written that, if the cellarer (steward) has to turn someone down for a request, he does so ever so kindly and always tries to at least give a kindly word. [2] We can also remember this attitude when speaking to anyone—an annoying neighbor, our difficult co-workers, even telephone marketing salespersons.

It is not important what these persons do to us so much as our guarding ourselves against sin. No matter how poorly someone may treat us let us be careful to see their unkindness as a real type of poverty. If we are as good as we can be we will be happy. Our sinning by a return of unkind words and actions only makes us unhappy and those who are unkind to us are feeding their own misery.

Let us also remember that attentiveness toward others is attentiveness to God. We cannot have one without the other. This is real prayer when we truly listen to those who are speaking to us and, conversely, it is an affront to God when we send one of his creatures abruptly out of our presence. This type of rude and impolite behavior can be a sign that we really don't believe that Jesus could return at any time.

When others are telling us something, whether it be our spouses, teachers, parents, children, or others, let us not be busy in our minds about what we are going to say in response. When we listen, let us "listen with the ear of our hearts" as Saint Benedict tells us in the prologue of his Rule, by letting others speak freely and deeply as though they were resting in the silence of our hearts, the silence of Christ dwelling in us. Let us not be too quick to respond unless it is necessary. Perhaps, it would be best if we allowed others to draw Christ's response from us by remembering Saint Benedict's advice on humility "by only speaking when asked a question." Allowing others to speak to us as another Christ brings about a deep sense of peace and communion. Likewise, we become more aware of what God is saying to us through others. When we are courteous and mindful of men, women, and children we are mindful of God. And therefore our interaction with others has become a prayer without ceasing (1 Thessalonians 5:17).

1. John Climacus: *Ladder of Divine Ascent*, p. 147.
2. *Rule of St. Benedict*, 31:6, 7.

✍ Chapter 23 ✍

Knowing the Will of God

We must, then, prepare our hearts and bodies
for the battle of holy obedience to his instructions.

RULE OF ST. BENEDICT, PROLOGUE: 40.

Knowing the will of God is difficult. We can never know that we are 100 percent in accord with the will of God. But as Thomas Merton wrote in his popular prayer, "I believe that the desire to please you [God] does in fact please you."

One of the surest ways to know that we are desiring God's will is to cheerfully do the will of those we love. I am not saying that we do not have opinions or that we are doormats. I am simply saying that God will work things out according to his plan. By striving to do all things in obedience we can keep our getting in the way of God's will to a minimum.

One thing that we can know for sure is that God wills us to be loving and kind to one another. If we love someone we will bind ourselves to them by being open to making their dreams and ideas come true as much as reasonably possible. God's plans will be accomplished if we spend our days in an attitude of love for God and neighbor. Jesus said, "But strive first for the kingdom of God and his righteousness, and all these things will be given to you as well" (Matthew 6:33).

Obedience is an intense kind of listening for the voice of God. Through obedience, the doors of our hearts are open and ready at the slightest command from God being mediated to us through others. Like Abraham, when we stay poised in an attitude of attentive obedience we are always available and waiting to say, "Here I am!" when the Lord speaks (Genesis 22:1).

Through obedience, we are always spiritually awake. When we insist on our own way we are, in a sense, becoming dull to the Holy Spirit and falling asleep. We become like the disciples falling asleep in the Garden of Gethsemani when they were disobedient to the Lord's request to "Remain here, and stay awake with me" (Matthew 26:38).

And let us not forget how costly the falling asleep of disobedience can be as it is recounted in the parable of the ten virgins. "As the bridegroom was delayed, all of them became drowsy and slept. . . ." The Lord said to them, "Truly I tell you, I do not know you" (Matthew 25: 1–13). Obedience is not a popular concept in our world today.

In the *Rule of St. Benedict* we read about the eleventh step of humility, which says that a person should speak only when asked a question. This may sound extreme but there is a good underlying principle at work. If we speak without anyone asking us to speak, how do we know that we are speaking according to God's will? If we answer another's questions out of love for that person, then we can be somewhat certain that the desire to "please God" is working within us.

This principle holds true for all of our actions if we do them from a spirit of obedience. This is what obedience and humility are all about, not beating ourselves up but truly seeking to be united to God by doing his will. It is all about desiring to please God every minute of every day out of a love and a longing to be united to him through others. With this love at work in us, our obedience becomes symbolic of the Holy Trinity, a type of deep converging of our will, God's will, and the will of those to whom we yield in obedience. Again, we make all of our actions a prayer without ceasing (1 Thessalonians 5:17).

Let us remember that Jesus would not have performed his first miracle at the wedding at Cana except for obedience to his mother, Mary, who asked him (John 2:1–11). If it is important to be obedient when performing something so great and good as a miracle, how much more important it is to be obedient in everyday matters.

What is best about obedience is the peace that becomes ours. Having freed our energies from getting stuck on our own desires, we are free to offer even more of our mental and willful attention to God in love. This leads us to an even deeper immersion in Christ and ultimately to a more profound experience of peace. Remember the Scripture passage, "Let them seek peace and pursue it" (1 Peter 3:11).

Having peace and following after it is the surest way of knowing that we are following Christ. Jesus also said, "Peace I leave with you; my peace I give to you" (John 14:27). When we act in obedience our conscience is not troubled and we experience deep peace. Even if we find ourselves in a dark or dry state of prayer, we will have a sense of peace knowing that we are in the darkness of faith.

Obedience, like the other ecumenical counsels (committing oneself to poverty, chastity, and obedience), is not a bondage but a liberation. Many of us hate the thought of being obedient to anyone. But we all realize that being obedient, as with civil laws, is freedom. For the most part, freedom is described in the context of the law, even the spiritual laws presented to us in the Word of God. Remember how Jesus said, "I did not come to abolish the law, but to fulfill the law." We must be careful to submit to the law in all areas. We should adhere to the Ten Commandments.

1. You shall have no other Gods before me. You shall not make for yourself an idol.
2. You shall not make wrongful use of the name of the Lord your God.
3. Remember the Sabbath day and make it holy.
4. Honor your mother and father.
5. You shall not murder.
6. You shall not commit adultery.
7. You shall not steal.
8. You shall not bear false witness against your neighbor.
9. You shall not covet your neighbor's wife.
10. You shall not covet your neighbor's house.

Obedience is a fact of everyday life. We can obediently unite ourselves more deeply to God and to others in little ways throughout our day. For example, when we are driving, we are obedient by not exceeding the speed limit, even if many are zooming by us. There are practical things that we can do each day to make yielding our will to others more palatable.

It will help us tremendously if we give ourselves plenty of time to get where we need to be. As much as possible, we can organize our time wisely in order not to get impatient. Hurrying can be a big cause of our forgetting proper behavior and wanting our own way. Knowing that God and others are always watching, let us seek to slow down so that we are aware of how we are behaving.

In other words, let our actions come from sound reason and careful thinking, rather than simply reacting to an outside stimulus. Let us strive never to give anyone reason to think ill of us and, if we do, let us promptly apologize for any wrong impression that we might have given. The Bible says, "For though they [the righteous] fall seven times, they will rise again" (Proverbs 24:16). It is not doing everything perfectly all the time that counts but maintaining our "desire to please God" in all that we say and do.

Anonymous Monks can often submit themselves to God through those who have some sort of authority over them. Remember how Jesus, when asked about whether people should pay their taxes or not, responded with this remark: "Give to Caesar what is Caesar's, and to God what is God's." Jesus submitted humbly to Pontius Pilate, knowing that God was fully in control despite Pilate's abuse of authority. Pontius Pilate said to Jesus, "Do you not know that I have power to release you and I have power to crucify you?"

Jesus revealed by his response the fact that God is in control of all things, that nothing can happen to us for which God does not have a purpose. Nothing can happen but that God does not approve, even if we may not understand the reasons until the next life. Jesus acknowledged the omnipotence of God when he responded to Pilate, "You would have no power over me unless it was given to you from above."

We need never feel as though we are victims. We need only to seek first the Kingdom of God and his righteousness, and everything else will fall into place. Those imprisoned should peacefully submit to those in authority. This does not mean that we should let people abuse us indefinitely, but simply that we should patiently and prudently seek God in all things, without acting impulsively. What we want is to avoid a knee-jerk reaction.

We may have to pray for years before we begin to feel called to action. We should refrain from making any major decisions until we are sure that God is calling us to do so. Until then, we should pray, pray, and pray with a genuine love for the good of all.

If there are situations that seem unjust, we must seek proper legal channels for dealing with the injustice. There are forums and meetings where we can share our differing opinions in an ordered way that can make a difference. I am speaking of organized gatherings, such as abortion forums and ecumenical forums, that are designed to promote the unity of world religions. We may learn something if we listen kindly to the opinions of others, even if they hold a position that is in sharp contrast to our own.

A spirit of flexibility permits us to change our plans somewhat if necessary. When we respond, we should avoid forcing our will upon others in a radical, emotional, and unreasonable way. (This is true in all situations, whether at home, work, church, or anywhere else.) We seek always to be in control of ourselves, our words, our tone of voice, volume, and body language. We try to always maintain proper decorum, especially when speaking of controversial topics.

Anonymous Monks with spouses can practice obedience by whole-heartedly giving themselves to their spouse in every aspect. Particularly in important matters, we will make every effort to check with our spouse by asking his or her opinion. Again, flexibility will help us to remain open to making changes in our plans in the event that we need to bend a little, in order to have agreement. Remember the Scripture passage in which Paul tells husbands and wives, "Be subject to one another out of reverence for Christ" (Ephesians 5:21).

Our obedience, like Saint Paul's, can lead others to Christ by our holy example. Remember how Paul obediently stayed in prison even after God miraculously opened the prison doors and, because he did so, the prison guard and all of his household came to faith in God (Acts 16:25–34).

Through humble obedience we become like little children, full of wonder and trust and possessing the freedom to have joyful fun and to be peacefully playful. "Whoever becomes humble like this child is the greatest in the kingdom of heaven" (Matthew 18:4).

I will close this chapter with the aforementioned prayer written by Thomas Merton in his book *Thoughts in Solitude*:

> My Lord God, I have no idea where I am going. I do not see the road ahead of me. I cannot know for certain where it will end. Nor do I really know myself, and the fact that I think that I am following your will does not mean that I am actually doing so. But I believe that the desire to please you does in fact please you. And I hope that I have that desire in all that I am doing. I hope that I will never do anything apart from that desire. And I know that if I do this you will lead me by the right road though I may know nothing about it. Therefore will I trust you always though I may seem to be lost and in the shadow of death. I will not fear, for you are ever with me, and you will never leave me to face my perils alone. (Farrar, Straus & Giroux, New York, 1958)

✍ Chapter 24 ✍
Sexual Relations Are Sacred

Hour by hour keep careful watch over all you do,
aware that God's gaze is upon you, wherever you may be.

RULE OF ST. BENEDICT, 4:48–49.

As Anonymous Monks with spouses we strive to be self-giving to one another as much as possible. This includes the total gift of oneself through loving sexual relations. I do not mean that we need to have sexual relations once a day, twice a day, every day, but simply that we should occasionally come together in physical union as an outward sign of our commitment to one another.

I have heard for some it can be more difficult to have sexual relations than to be a celibate. Often, when hormones are drying up and spouses are physically and emotionally distant, it can be a real sacrifice to offer oneself to one's spouse in sexual relations. This is particularly true for those whose spouses are often irritable.

Those who feel this way should try not to think about whether their spouse deserves to have sexual relations with them or not. Let us consider following the good example of Jesus who allows all to partake of him when they receive him in the Eucharist, even though many do not deserve him.

With the help of God's grace, we can act the same way with our spouses. We will experience making a true unconditional gift of ourselves in this way. If you are not able to make such a gift at this time, try to be open to what God can accomplish in your life. Remember that we can do all things through Christ who gives us strength (Philippians 4:13).

(I do not condone forced sex—that borders on rape. Nor do I condone fornication, incest, homosexuality, or anything of the sort. The advice on marriage given here is intended only for those persons who are in a valid sacramental marriage.)

Ideally, the husband and wife both agree on how often sexual relations will take place, and what is done during these times. If your spouse wants you to do something sexually that you are really not comfortable with, pray for your spouse and explain that you are not comfortable with the act. In love and true concern for the happiness of your spouse, seek out other ways to have sexual relations that will be equally pleasing, ways that you can both agree on. When there is strong disagreement concerning what is and what is not sexually acceptable, it may be necessary to talk to a qualified therapist or counselor.

Many marriages have broken apart because of unhappy sexual relations. Sexual relations affirm the fact that we are never truly separated from our spouse and remind us that we truly have become "one body" in Christ. I would also like to add that attentiveness during sexual relations is very much like our attentiveness toward God during prayer—our entire focus is fixed on the present moment.

Couples often fall silent during sexual experiences, much like the sacred silence that takes place during wordless (apophatic) prayer. Our mental state during peak moments of sexual arousal is similar to the peak moments of prayer—when the mind is completely at rest, our minds are still, and seemingly inactive.

This union between ourselves and our spouse represents the peak union of humankind's spiritual union with God. This is why we hear so many beautiful sexual overtones in the great story of God and his beloved church, the greatest of love stories, the Song of Songs.

Whether we enjoy sex or not, physical sexual union, like celibacy, can be a source of grace that contributes to the salvation of the Anonymous Monk, of one's spouse, family, those in purgatory, and the whole world.

Chapter 25

Making Fashion a Prayer

Your way of acting should be different from the world's way;
the love of Christ must come before all else.

RULE OF ST. BENEDICT, 4:20–21.

🌀A s I have mentioned throughout this book, we seek to make everything a prayer. From the food we eat to the clothes we wear, everything has some element of God. Below are a few suggestions that will help make even our choice of clothing a prayer. Take what you like and leave the rest. Each one creates an image of themselves that they present to others.

God has an image of each of us that he wants us to live out fully, even in our dress. As Anonymous Monks, we should reflect this true image, which is an image that speaks of depth, mental and emotional stability, modesty, integrity, and piety.

There are many stories about saintly persons who spoke to others about God simply by their appearance. I am not talking about a superficial appearance that encompasses merely someone's clothing, hair color, nail polish, or the type of car they drive. I am speaking of a holy presence or aura that radiates from the very countenance of a person, as was said of many of the saints. Perhaps it is our appearance that reflects the amount of time that we spend with God in prayer.

People usually present the image that they feel most comfortable with, unless, because of upbringing or peer pressure, one dresses in order to conform, to fit in. I have heard of persons who continually dressed in a certain manner even though they did not feel comfortable doing so, just because society, the media, or magazines had conveyed to them that this was the way they should look. In our day, it is often considered fashionable to dress in an immodest way, a way that usually exploits women, a way that implies that women are good for only one thing.

As long as we exploit ourselves by presenting ourselves as objects to be longed for and used, we will never realize our true human capacity or the highest creative good that we can bring to society. When we overemphasize looking good, sexy, and physically attractive, not only do we distract others from realizing their true level of good, but we distract ourselves from fully blossoming as intellectual, creative, productive human beings.

I include in this admonition going overboard with physical exercises, so that our bodies appear to be sleek and trim. We exercise to stay healthy. Contrary to popular belief, we don't have to be a perfect ten. "[W]hile physical training is of some value, godliness [spiritual training] is valuable in every way" (1 Timothy 4:8).

I will again use Albert Einstein as an example, because one look at Albert Einstein will tell you that this was a man who put all of his energy into thinking and not outward appearances. If we want to be leaders, be it spiritual, social, or political, we have to dress like leaders. If we believe that our identity is in God and not things, we have to look like our identity is in God. This does not mean that we have to dress like monks and nuns, but at the same time we have to realize that we may not be taken seriously if we exploit our own selves by the way we present ourselves to others.

I am including a few suggestions, especially for women, to help find balance in the area of proper appearance for Anonymous Monks. Take what you like and leave the rest. You will find that much of what is written below does not apply to men. Men don't have to dye their hair, wear make up and nail polish, or shave their legs and underarms to be taken seriously—why should women? Women can stand upon the intellectual gifts and talents that God has given them, just like men.

The austerities I present may help us to take some of the love that we have for ourselves and our appearance, and dedicate that love wholeheartedly to the service of God alone. The less attention we pay to ourselves, the more attention we can pay to God. We can also more fully unite ourselves to the poor, imprisoned, and sick, because many of the things mentioned below are usually things that the poor, imprisoned, and sick naturally have to do or do without.

Consider these suggestions as warnings or pitfalls that some of us who have a tendency toward vanity may fall into, pitfalls that can become a sort of self-glorification, if we are not careful. The fact that many may not be willing to let go of the practices mentioned below only shows the grip that they have on us:

1. As Anonymous Monks, we can try to use little if any makeup, perfume, cologne, fingernail polish, hair dyes, or jewelry, except for wedding rings and religious articles like medals. [1]

2. To avoid the strong attachment and love that many have for their hair, we can consider hairstyles that are plain and simple (1 Peter 3:3), preferably cut short or worn up for women and no longer than the shoulders for men (1 Corinthians 11:14). (Anonymous Monks may even want to shave their heads.)

3. We can choose simpler clothing. [2] All skirts and dresses could be below the knee. We could consider not wearing shorts in public, but, if they must be worn, let them be the long kind, cut just above the knee. If one must wear a swimsuit, try a one-piece, perhaps using a coverall or T-shirt. It's a good idea for clothing to have a loose or tailored fit. Ideally our shoes will be flat, not elevator or high-heeled shoes. [3]

4. If possible, Anonymous Monks, men and women, might consider not shaving their bodies at all. Many women, especially outside the United States, do not shave.

A nonymous Monks do not condemn others who do any of the things listed above. We do not consider such practices bad in themselves, but simply not conducive to monastic living. If someone in authority, or a spouse, insists on continuing some of the above practices, the Anonymous Monk should concede in order to keep the peace. Eventually, with prayer, things may change.

At the same time, Anonymous Monks are not deliberately trying to be repulsive and offensive. The virtue in this matter of good grooming is to shun artificiality and to cultivate the beauty that radiates naturally from within a pure heart. As Saint Peter says, "Do not adorn yourselves outwardly by braiding your hair, and by wearing gold ornaments or fine clothing; rather let your adornment be the inner self with the lasting beauty of a gentle and quiet spirit, which is very precious in God's sight" (1 Peter 3:3–4).

1. Tertullian: "The Apparel of Women."
2. *Trappist Constitution*, ch. 21.
3. Tertullian, "The Apparel of Women."

🖉 Chapter 26 🖳
Caring for the
Sick Prayerfully

[The] sick must be patiently borne with,
because serving them leads to a greater reward.
RULE OF ST. BENEDICT, 36:5.

🖳P ersons with incapacitating and chronic physical or mental illness have much value to God and to the entire world. By the effects of their illness many are forced to live lives of great sacrifice. Like the abandoned Christ, they are also abandoned with no one to love them, no one to care for them.

In the eyes of many, they are to be thrown out like the trash. Many physically and mentally imperfect people are thrown out even by the ones who are supposed to love them the most, their own family. "And whoever does not provide for relatives and especially family members has denied the faith and is worse than an unbeliever" (1 Timothy 5:8).

If we have an opportunity to care for sick children or aged parents, let's do so with kindness, gentleness, and patience—the same way that we would want to be treated. Sometimes, it can be very difficult to tend to others, especially if we are awakened in the middle of the night and we have to work the next day.

Once, in the middle of the night, my entire family (five persons besides myself) was extremely sick and vomiting. There was vomit everywhere, down the hall, on the bedclothes, and all over the walls. Listening to everyone groan and agonize with nausea was frightening, but at the same time I was very grateful to God that I was well enough to take care of them and to clean up after them. I joyfully cleaned up all the vomit and gave thanks to God that he left at least one of us to tend to the others who were sick.

When a neighbor or someone we know is sick (this includes pregnant women), we try to prepare food for them, shop for groceries, clean their house, do their laundry, or offer to spend quality time with their children. This is especially important if the person or persons are terminally ill.

I once had a friend (I'll call her Joan) who was dying of leukemia. Our children attended school together so we would carpool. When it was Joan's teenage son's birthday, I filled my van with helium balloons. When I went to pick up the boy from school, I pushed the balloons out of the van and everyone yelled, "Happy Birthday!" The entire school was waiting outside and everyone saw the attention that the boy was getting. I even bought some small gifts and told the boy that the balloons and gifts were from his mother and her idea. When the boy arrived home from school he telephoned his mother (she was dying in an out-of-state hospital). The boy laughed and joyfully thanked his mother repeatedly for the great birthday surprise.

Later Joan, who was now very sick, wrote me a letter. Her hand-writing was very shaky and faint. She wrote, "You are truly a Christian. Thank you for giving me the credit for my son's birthday surprise." I was touched by the note but I didn't have the courage to tell Joan that the reason behind my helping was the fact that I had once turned my back on a husband and wife with AIDS.

Out of fear of contracting AIDS or of one of my own children getting the disease, I had kept away from this couple. Feeling remorseful, I was now determined to make up for my past indifference and never to discriminate against sick persons again. This was the reason for my kindness toward Joan and her family.

Let us offer to help in any way. Using prudence, we can be careful that we don't go overboard and become a nuisance and possibly interfere. Families with very sick members often need private time to grieve and reflect.

We don't have to pretend to understand totally the pain that the terminally ill or their loved ones are going through. We can be careful not to offer pat answers or to try to talk them out of their suffering—doing so can sound as if we are trying to minimize their suffering. Sometimes, we wrongfully try to talk people out of their suffering or even blame them for their illness (as people often do to smokers with cancer).

We realize that grieving is an intense form of contemplation that leaves a person clinging to God for strength and hope. We may be acting selfishly without realizing it if we do not want to pay attention to another's suffering. We may feel the need to think of reasons that they deserve their sickness in order to justify God not healing them. The misery of their suffering can even seem to be an interruption of our lives.

By our actions we can be sending the message that their suffering is a burden and interruption that we just don't want to deal with. This is the type of behavior that we read about in the Book of Job concerning his so-called friends. These friends were convinced that Job must have done something wrong to cause his suffering. It is wise for anyone who is experiencing great loss of any kind to read the entire Book of Job thoroughly and prayerfully.

Let us also remember the great care and respect that we should extend to the elderly in every way. Remember that wonderful exhortation to love the elderly given us by Saint Benedict when he says: "Whenever brothers meet, the junior asks his senior for a blessing. When an older monk comes by, the younger rises and offers him a seat, and does not presume to sit unless the older bids him. In this way, they do what the words of Scripture say: 'They should each try to be the first to show respect to the other' " (Romans 12:10). [1]

We are in a constant state of change from the moment we are conceived. All the changes in our lives are by God's design including aging. Watching ourselves and others grow old is an exciting and mysterious event. Our aging is as mysterious as a giant oak developing from one small acorn. What a mystery! Aging has a hold of us and will not let go—men and women in all humankind deepening with age. As we age we become more and more beautiful. Our beauty lies in our evolution.

I know that this goes against what the world and the media says about aging. Our world often does not appreciate the elderly but to God the aged are ever more and more beautiful. If this was not true there would be no aging. The elderly have changed from their youth and they continue to evolve with all the magnificence of God's creation. Our elderly are beautiful, lovely, and deep because God remembers them since they were in their mother's womb. God sees the whole person and knows that their loveliness lies in their evolution: changing, growing, developing, until death. What a good and merciful God that we have in allowing us to age. "Gray hair is a crown of glory" (Psalm 16:31).

A nonymous Monks are careful to take care of their own health by getting all the necessary preventative checkups. Going to the doctor can give us a great sense of peace. We can have the assurance that we are doing all that we can, instead of worrying about what the doctor might discover.

I knew a man who was nauseous all the time. He was afraid to go to the doctor. He was afraid the doctor would tell him that he had cancer. Well, the man continued to get worse. When he did finally go to the doctor, the doctor did tell him that he had cancer. Now he has to go to the doctor on a regular basis but it is too late for the doctors to do anything because he waited too long. So it does not do us any good to ignore our health.

Manual labor is a big part of the daily schedule in many monastic communities. Therefore, monks can often be assured of physical exercise. However, those of us who have jobs that do not require physical exertion may decide to do some jogging or other exercise to stay in shape. Human beings consist of spirit, mind, and body. It is a good idea for us to exercise each of these areas of our humanity each day by praying, reading, and physical exertion. But let us not overdo physical exercise. We should count our spiritual exercise as having the greater value because the rewards are eternal.

Many people do not realize that physical exercise is mentioned in the Bible. "Train yourself in godliness, for, while physical training is of some value, godliness is valuable in every way, holding promise for both the present life and the life to come" (1 Timothy 4:8). I have also read that gymnasiums were constructed centuries ago specifically to keep men away from the things of God. The "gymnasium" is mentioned in

Catholic Bibles in 1 Maccabees 1:14. Commenting on this passage, the Catholic World Press version of the American Bible states: "Gymnasium: symbol and center of athletic and intellectual life, it was the chief Hellenistic propaganda. Jewish youth were attracted by sports and encouraged to join youth clubs. They received training in military skills and the duties of citizens. Through the participation of the intellectual life many were won to paganism" (p. 469).

Monks in a monastery live by a schedule throughout their day called the *horarium*. The schedule of prayer, work, and spiritual reading that we develop over time becomes our spiritual gym, our spiritual workout. Like an athlete, our challenge is to strive to adhere to our private *horarium* as much as possible.

Anonymous Monks who are sick may take frequent baths and showers, if necessary. Those who enjoy good health can try to limit themselves to a reasonable period of time and avoid basking for long periods in luxurious baths. [2] It may help to realize that the poor, imprisoned, and chronically ill can rarely, if ever, enjoy a warm bath. Therefore, we can practice solidarity with the poor, imprisoned, and sick by this small sacrifice of foregoing luxurious baths and showers.

As Anonymous Monks we can further unite ourselves to the poor by forgoing the use of air conditioning and heating unless it not to do so would severely hurt our health or the health of others. I have friends who are poor. Poor people who live in very hot climates often cannot afford air conditioning. Living like the poor keeps us mindful of the financially poor, emotionally poor, and the poor in spirit.

Our thoughts for the poor, which are brought on by our imitation of them, are a source of union and strength for all the world. Our prayers are more effective if we live like the poor rather than praying for the poor from on high. Otherwise, we seem to be like the rich man who distanced himself from the poor beggar Lazarus by his comforts and thoughtlessness. The rich man stayed in his cozy and fancy house while Lazarus suffered severely in the street. When they both died the roles were reversed and now it was the disdained Lazarus who was comforted by God while the rich man was in torment (Luke 19).

I am not trying to make anyone feel guilty for having much. I am saying that we can try to avoid relishing in comforts by tempering ourselves with moderate use. Let us unite ourselves to all those who are suffering by living simply and humbly as the sick, poor, and oppressed are forced to do. This is one of the best ways to visit Jesus in the sick, by joining ourselves to them by our common sacrifices.

1. *Rule of St. Benedict*, 63:15–17.
2. *Rule of St. Benedict*, 36:8.

ᔥ Chapter 27 ᔥ
Give and You Will Receive

[We] must show every care and concern for the sick, children, guests and the poor, knowing for certain that [we] will be held accountable for all of them on the day of judgment.
RULE OF ST. BENEDICT, 31:9.

When using our occupational gifts and talents, let us remember that the true purpose of our employment is for the betterment and service of humankind. Let's try to refrain from becoming money-motivated by letting our employment be reduced to nothing more than a pastime driven by capital. If we are doctors, let us nurture good health for love of God and neighbor. If we are entertainers or restaurateurs, let our objective be simply providing pleasure and enjoyment for others.

Let us seek to obtain the humility and sharing attitude that says, I am in need of others and others are in need of me. All work, no matter how seemingly insignificant, is important to society. This realization truly binds us together as brothers and sisters. We develop a deep and lasting dependency on one another that is symbolic of the Holy Trinity itself. Remember in the Book of Acts how "There was not a needy person among them, for as many as owned lands or houses sold them and brought the proceeds of what was sold. They laid it at the apostles' feet, and it was distributed to each as any had need" (Acts 4:34–35). This sharing binds us together in deep love.

In regards to payment for our services, let us remember the Scripture passage, "You received without payment, give without payment"

(Matthew 10:8). Many of us have received the gifts of sight, sound, touch, health, intellect, and the ability to learn. These are all free gifts that have been given to us by God and are at the core and foundation of all of our occupational achievements.

As Anonymous Monks we are willing and open to take donations for our services and products and we are willing to work for free for those who cannot afford to pay. If we act in this way we can be sure that when we are in need we will be helped. Jesus makes this promise to us, "Give, and it will be given to you. A good measure, packed down, shaken together, running over, will be put into your lap; for the measure you give will be the measure you get back" (Luke 6:38).

We must be careful not to turn away those in need, especially those of us who are doctors, dentists, clothing manufacturers, those in food service, ministers and teachers of the gospel and the spiritual life, and other occupations that address the most basic and crucial needs. Let us remember the Scripture passage, "From everyone to whom much has been given, much will be required; and from the one to whom much has been entrusted, even more will be demanded" (Luke 12:48).

The Scriptures also say, "Laborers deserve their food" (Matthew 10:10) and social justice would surely dictate that everyone should make a decent wage as so many, especially teachers in our day, are far underpaid. So I am not against persons making money, but I am urging against the accumulation of money as our only motivation for the work and services that we offer.

If we insist on payment for everything that we do, we miss out on achieving a deep spiritual union with others that incorporates us into the one body, the one family in Christ. If we refuse to do anything unless we are paid, we needlessly cut ourselves off from others and reduce ourselves to nothing more than a "hired hand" (John 10:12–15).

Generosity comes in many forms, such as spending time with someone that we may find boring, smiling to our neighbor, or praying for the world. We can also be generous by speaking politely, encouraging others, providing food, clothing, and furniture.

A nonymous Monks, using prudence, will be generously willing to share all that we have, especially with the poor. If we see a beggar, we should give a little something if we are able, even if we can only give a smile or a kind word. Remember, Saint Francis of Assisi was also a beggar, and it takes humility to beg.

When it comes to giving a few pennies or dollars, do not judge, give freely. Remember that we all have received freely from the hand of God (Matthew 10:8). You may think to yourself that the beggar is a bum and not working, but, for some, begging is work, and it's better than doing nothing. Besides, begging is so humbling that most of us would not be willing to do it. For this, the beggar is to be commended. We cannot assume that the beggar will be out buying liquor with our donation. However, if we do see a beggar in a drunken stupor, it would be better not to give him any money.

We should be especially considerate of the needs of those who share our faith (Galatians 6:10). If we have knowledge of someone in need, and we have the ability to help, we should try to share (James 2:16). When it comes to relatively large commitments or commitments on an ongoing basis, we must be prudent and give only what we feel totally comfortable with, not giving out of compulsion or coercion.

In regard to those living in our own household, we should have the attitude of "sharing all things in common" (Acts 2:44). As Saint Therese of the Little Way has said, we should try not to use the word "mine," but rather "ours." There may be times when we are expected to support relatives who are not among our immediate family members. In this case, we can use Joseph with the coat of many colors from the Old Testament as our role model (Genesis 37).

Joseph took care of his brothers, even after they had sold him as a slave. We should also be willing to help our family members, if we are able, no matter what they may have done to us (Genesis 50:19–21).

When it comes to unruly, irresponsible family members who have shown no sign of remorse, it is helpful to remember that Joseph, using prudence, did not help his brothers until he had first tested them to see if they had had a change of heart (Genesis 42–45).

I am saying this because in promoting generosity I am not condoning throwing money to the wind by continually supporting someone who shows no sign of changing for the better, for example, alcoholics, drug addicts, and lazy types who would be better off if they were forced to help themselves. We should refrain from doing for others what they should be doing for themselves. Sometimes, it is simply more prudent not to help someone financially, because they will not return to God until they end up at the pig trough like the prodigal son (Luke 15:11–32). In modern words, we should not enable them; they need to hit rock bottom.

We should have a genuine love and pity for alcoholics, drug addicts, prostitutes, and the like. They suffer from very low esteem of themselves and their value to God. I have heard that police are now taking video cameras instead of guns into drug-infested neighborhoods. There, they videotape those who are drunk or on drugs. Then they show the tape to the person when they catch them sober. Many have been shocked into sobriety having seen themselves as others truly see them. So let's pray and be patient that one day all may discover that they are truly valued children of God.

In keeping with generosity, we should not hesitate to offer a small donation to our postal and sanitary workers, at least once a year. When we see our garbage man or postman, we should offer them a cold drink when it is hot, or a hot drink when it is cold, remembering that they are a blessing to us throughout the year. If we have maintenance men, roofers, landscapers, snow removal servicemen, etc., working at our homes or offices, we should offer them refreshment. (Alcoholic beverages would not be appropriate while they are working or if they will be driving.)

Anonymous Monks should not lend out things if we are concerned about getting them back. Once someone has borrowed something from us, we must not be overly concerned about getting it back.

Using prudence, we should also have a last will and testament for the purpose of generously and properly dispersing our belongings after our death. And along the same lines, a living will and a durable power of attorney are useful for medical purposes.

☙ Chapter 28 ☙
The Value of Suffering

First and foremost, there must be no word or sign of the evil
of grumbling, no manifestation of it for any reason at all.
RULE OF ST. BENEDICT, 34:6.

E arlier in the book, I referred to a quote from Thomas Merton concerning love. Merton wrote in *Love and Living*, "The question of love is one that cannot be evaded. Whether or not you claim to be interested in it, from the moment you are alive you are bound to be concerned with love, because love is not just something that happens to you: it is a certain way of being alive."

As a preface to this chapter, I would like to take out the word "love" and exchange it with the word "suffering" so that the it now reads: "The question of *suffering* is one that cannot be evaded. Whether or not you claim to be interested in it, from the moment you are alive you are bound to be concerned with *suffering*, because *suffering* is not just something that happens to you: it is a certain way of being alive." Everyone is suffering in some area of their lives, be it moral suffering (the suffering that comes from doing the right thing), emotional suffering, suffering from mental or physical illness, financial suffering, suffering from sour relationships with others, and so on. Do we really want to run from all suffering? I think not, because it is most definitely true that suffering is a certain way of being "alive."

As Anonymous Monks we come to realize that suffering is a prayer, a mediation, and a positive action of the Holy Spirit to aid us toward union with God. According to the *Merriam-Webster Dictionary*, the word "suffering" means "to feel or endure pain, misery, or hardship." Suffering in itself is not really the problem, but rather our negative perception of the various events and hardships that take place in our lives and in the lives of others.

Something that can really help us in our perception of suffering is to think eternally or to be eternally minded. If we believe that this world as we know it is the only life, then we will most definitely think of our lives as David did when he said, "The days of our life are seventy years, or perhaps eighty, if we are strong; even then their span is only toil and trouble; they are soon gone, and we fly away" (Psalm 90:10).

Moses went through tremendous adversity while leading the Israelites to the Promised Land. However, he had a vision of the place and the life to come that kept him going in good form. If we, like Moses, look at all of our suffering as preparation for the life to come, then we can more readily allow ourselves to be purified by suffering's molding and refining action. And this includes when others inflict suffering on us.

When we die and see God's glory, any wrong that was ever perpetrated against us will dissolve into insignificance. God's glory is so spectacular that we will wish for everyone to share it, even those most seemingly hardened criminals. In the presence of God's glory nothing in this life, good or bad, will matter. We will surely want to be one with all, forever enjoying God's love.

Often, there is suffering that seems to overwhelm us. Nothing that anyone can say or do can give us comfort. Suffering has taken a hold of us and will not let us go until we become pliable, open, accepting, and willing to yield under the hand of our almighty Father. It matters little how our suffering has come upon us.

We could blame ourselves or we could blame others indefinitely, but this is not where the real flexibility lies. God's love in us does not brood over injury or wrongs done to us (1 Corinthians 13:5). Our unwillingness to yield to love is its own record. As we yield and repent of our own defiance and bitterness we aid God in removing the obstacles that block his love in us. David committed many serious sins, sins of adultery and murder, but yet when the prophet corrected him he immediately admitted his error (2 Samuel 12:13). I think that this is a very big reason why God called David a man after his own heart.

Saints do not pretend never to have made a mistake, nor do they have an exaggerated sense of guilt. We can experience remorse and contrition as David did, but we must not judge and eternally condemn ourselves or others. This condemning ourselves can be pride—pride in the sense that we have judged ourselves rather than allow God to be our judge. We can actually be placing ourselves above God when we say, I will not be forgiven. This is not for us to decide. Paul says, "I do not even judge myself" (1 Corinthians 4:3).

I once had a baby boy die four months into my pregnancy. I blamed myself severely for the miscarriage because I had lifted some heavy rocks while doing some lawn work. We have to remember that it is human nature that we place blame on ourselves or on others. I think this is why Jesus mentions the incident of the tower at Siloam falling and killing eighteen people. Jesus said, "Or those eighteen who were killed when the tower of Siloam fell on them—do you think that they were worse offenders than all the others living in Jerusalem? No, I will tell you; but unless you repent, you will all parish just as they did" (Luke 13:4–5).

As Jesus said, the most important thing that any one of us can do when we are suffering is to repent. Suffering has a way of causing us to be sober in our actions, thoughts, and speech. This is what I think Jesus means when he is calling for us to repent. It does not necessarily mean that we are breaking the Ten Commandments; it simply means that we need to think eternally. "Am I ready to meet God? Am I making a big deal over grievances, hardship, and misfortune when what I really need to do is be a loving friend to those around me, including myself?"

Suffering can bring entire communities together in peace and sobriety. It always amazes me that when a tragedy like a hurricane or earthquake occurs, all prejudice and ego subsides as all focus turns to the care and concern and well-being of the victims. I do not mean to minimize the pain of those of us who suffer, but I can say that when we see where our sufferings leads us, if we do not despair and we persevere in love, we will see all the good that comes as a result.

When we suffer let us try not to feel too sorry for ourselves. "My brothers and sisters, whenever you face trials of any kind, consider it nothing but joy, because you know that the testing of your faith produces endurance; and let endurance have its full effect, so that you may be mature and complete, lacking in nothing" (James 1:2–4).

In our suffering we are not alone. Everyone who ever lived has suffered in some area of their life, be it physical, emotional, mental, or financial. Remember the Scripture passage concerning our brothers and sisters who also suffer. "Discipline yourselves, keep alert. Like a roaring lion your adversary the devil prowls around, looking for someone to devour. Resist him, steadfast in your faith, for you know that your brothers and sisters in all the world are undergoing the same kinds of suffering" (1 Peter 5:8–9).

When we have suffered a severe loss, such as the loss of health, or the loss of a loved one, or our dignity, or our finances, let us not get bitter. The choice is ours. I once heard the wife of a Protestant preacher, who also had a baby die, say, "We can get bitter or better."

When we suffer we can cling to God with all our heart, mind, and strength, remaining utterly dependent on him to see us through, one minute at a time. Suffering can help us to reach the higher levels of love by ridding us of excess baggage in the same way that mountain climbers can reach higher peaks by ridding themselves of unnecessary supplies. If we relinquish always being comfortable, if we step up to the challenge of allowing ourselves to go beyond mere human thinking, we will become agile and flexible. Pain and suffering will no longer cause us to be sad. Instead, we will rejoice because we will have overcome our sufferings through the love of Christ; we will have overcome the world.

Some saints, if you can imagine, were actually sad if they did not have something to suffer each day. Suffering can mean that we are hurting so that others might live. Jesus suffered and we know that a servant is never greater than his or her master. No matter what our suffering is, we can relate it to some aspect of the life of Jesus, Mary, and the saints.

When we accept our sufferings with an open heart we are truly eternally minded. We begin to realize the strength that God has given us. We become convinced that God is real because we know that it is not humanly possible for us to withstand many of the sufferings that we have experienced. Our perseverance in suffering gives us proof that we truly love God more than anything.

By our perseverance we tell God that we love him above all things. We experience the beauty of a union of our own free will and God's will. There is a beautiful submission, something like the marital union, that takes place when we yield to all adversity, when we yield to the God whose power and mind is beyond human understanding. God's immenseness, God's majesty sweeps over us like lovers. We yield to God without relying on analysis. Our docility and lucidity in the Bridegroom's hands leaves us meek, mild, and peaceful. Our deep love is based on who he is, not on what we are getting or not getting.

This love is not based on what we keep or lose; it is based on God who is eternal. In all of our sufferings we learn to say, "The LORD gave, and the LORD has taken away; blessed be the name of the LORD" (Job 1:21). This is what suffering helps us to achieve, the freedom to live in the love of God where loss cannot touch us. "Where, O death, is your sting?" (1 Corinthians 15:55).

Having had to endure much suffering, we rise to the state of love where we will always be. Where nothing can be taken way, where nothing can separate us from the love of God (Romans 8:35). What freedom!

In life we often hear of "has beens." People who once excelled in a particular field and now they have been passed by and forgotten. God, on the other hand, is referred to in Scripture as the great "I Am." The God who is and was and will always be. When we, like Moses, focus our attention on the life to come, we will always be, we will continually grow in that science that will always be, the science of love. We have the freedom and liberty to never worry about being a "has been." "I am" and I will always be a child of God and no amount of suffering can ever take that away. What unshakable confidence! What eternal security!

A s Jesus sought to discern the will of God in the Garden of Gethsemani, Anonymous Monks also use prudence to discern the meaning of their sufferings. Jesus prayed (Mark 14:36) and asked God to remove his impending suffering (his crucifixion). So it is not wrong for us to pray and ask God to take away our suffering. Ultimately, God always does what is best for our souls and the souls of others. In the case of Jesus' crucifixion, it apparently was better for him to suffer so that he could be eternally exalted and we along with him.

Similarly, Saint Paul also prayed three times for God to remove the "thorn . . . given me in the flesh" (2 Corinthians 12:7). No one is sure what this affliction was. It could have been a physical or spiritual affliction. Either way, God responded to Paul with, "My grace is sufficient for you" (2 Corinthians 12:8). Paul's afflictions apparently were not leaving him but God promised to give Paul the grace to handle whatever problems he encountered. God will also do the same for us. God will give us what we need each day.

Here is an elementary example of our using prudence and prayer. If an Anonymous Monk has a headache, he or she should do whatever is necessary to relieve his or her suffering. However, if it turns out to be an incurable ailment and everything has been done, including persistent prayer, and the condition still persists, then he or she may have to come to the realization that God's grace is sufficient. In other words, their strength to deal with their suffering is itself an answer to prayer. Most persons will discover that, with the help of God's grace, they can endure far more suffering than they think.

No matter what we suffer or why, we can offer the energy of our suffering to God for the salvation of the entire world. We can truly thank God that we are counted worthy to suffer in the name of Jesus (Acts 5:41). Saint Paul said, "I am now rejoicing in my sufferings for your sake, and in my flesh I am completing what is lacking in Christ's for the sake of his body, that is, the church" (Colossians 1:24).

"Who are these, robed in white, and where have they come from? . . . These are they who have come out of the great ordeal; they have washed their robes and made them white in the blood of the lamb. For this reason they are before the throne of God, and worship him day and night within his temple" (Revelation 7:13–15).

Chapter 29

Being Spiritual
Is Not Being Stupid

*"Do everything with counsel and you will
not be sorry afterward" (Sirach 32:24).*
RULE OF ST. BENEDICT, 3:13.

If Anonymous Monks experience strong intuitive feelings, worldly joy, or romantic longings we try not to let these feelings override our intellect. [1] For instance, it is not wise to quit going to our medical doctor simply because we feel that we have enough faith and don't need our doctor anymore. Anyone with a serious physical problem should seek advice from a medical doctor; someone with a financial problem should seek help from a financial expert; and those with marital problems should seek the assistance of a marriage counselor.

Anonymous Monks will not substitute spiritual advice for medical advice, marital counseling, or financial advice. They will act according to prudence, which means that they take the proper measures in order to care for themselves. In other words, prudence allows us to "discern our true good in every circumstance." [2]

Also, in regards to the above-mentioned false joys and romantic longings, Anonymous Monks try not to allow themselves to follow feelings that do not result in a deeper, more dedicated commitment to God. [3] We are careful to maintain regular fellowship with those persons who spur us on to holiness.

Relationships that distract or seduce us away from a deeper love for God may have to be temporarily avoided, especially if there are sexual implications. Perhaps, we can go back to the relationship later when we are stronger. I am talking about relationships that could result in an illicit sexual union. For various reasons many are vulnerable to acts of fornication. Some persons struggle with thoughts of fornication their entire lives.

If we experience this type of temptation it may be that we have not yet learned how to love others in a deep spiritual sense. If we are physically attracted to a particular person, we may have the habit of automatically fantasizing about having sexual relations with them. With the help of God's grace, along with our sincere desire to strive to love perfectly, our attractions to others become a result of our spiritual attraction to Christ. We then experience a spiritual union that is much deeper than any physical union. Through holy living, we can touch others much more deeply than any person could ever touch another physically.

Many spiritual persons have fooled themselves by harboring unholy feelings of lust in so-called friendships, pointing out that Jesus himself had close fellowship with some women. This is true. However, Jesus' close relationships with persons of the opposite sex were relationships in which everyone involved was focused on God. Jesus addressed these women on his way to the crucifixion (Luke 23:27). This tells us that it is okay to have deep spiritual friendships as long as we love God, and the accomplishment of his will first and foremost.

Spiritual union with others is lasting and deep but for many of us learning to love on a spiritual level can take time. I am also talking about women experiencing a deep spiritual love for women and men experiencing a deep spiritual love for men. Remember how deeply Jesus cared for John, his beloved disciple. How John laid his head on the chest of Jesus at the Last Supper.

Let's also consider the great love David had for Jonathan when he wrote, "I am distressed for you, my brother Jonathan; greatly beloved were you to me; your love to me was wonderful, passing the love of women" (2 Samuel 1:26). We should not be afraid to allow ourselves to love and to touch others as John loved and touched Jesus and as David clearly loved Jonathan. As Anonymous Monks, we need not appear rigid or less than human. Remember that in Christ even our very souls touch, having become one in him.

In today's society if a person finds himself or herself falling in love with someone of the same sex, he or she almost automatically assumes that these are homosexual tendencies and that there is something wrong with him or her. We can learn to have deep, loving, beautiful relationships with men and women as long as we do so out of love for Christ.

This is another reason why it is always good to discuss our inner thoughts with our spiritual director or companion. Letting others take a close look at our thoughts and feelings will help us to see our relationships more clearly and keep us from acting on impulses that are not spiritually edifying. Also, we must remember that if we have a strong attraction to someone we could completely destroy this relationship by making inappropriate remarks and advances. We don't want that.

We want to discern what is good and retain it. "Beloved, do not believe every spirit, but test the spirits to see whether they are from God; for many false prophets have gone out into the world. By this you know the Spirit of God: every spirit that confesses that Jesus Christ has come in the flesh is from God, and every spirit that does not confess Jesus is not from God. And this is the spirit of the antichrist" (1 John 4:1–3).

If we can have a discussion with someone that we are attracted to about our love for Jesus on a deep level, this will help us to stay focused and chaste in that relationship. If, when we speak of Jesus, that person flees, then we know that Christ has been rejected and there is no real true relationship there. "We are from God. Whoever knows God listens to us, and whoever is not from God does not listen to us. From this we know the spirit of truth and the spirit of error" (1 John 4:6).

I am not saying that we scratch anyone out of our lives. We simply continue to love each person by our holy example without getting tangled in feelings of the flesh, in feelings of lust. The name of Jesus is very powerful and I have seen it happen many times that demons flee at his holy name.

If we still have doubts about our sincerity to serve God in our relationships with others, let's remember the advice of God himself in the chapter from Sacred Scripture about holiness in sexual conduct (1 Thessalonians 4:3–8). "For this is the will of God, your sanctification:

that you abstain from fornication; that each one of you know how to control your own body in holiness and honor, not with lustful passion like the Gentiles who do not know God; that no one wrong or exploit a brother or sister in this matter, because the Lord is an avenger in all these things, just as we have already told you beforehand and solemnly warned you. For God did not call us to impurity but in holiness. Therefore whoever rejects this, rejects not human authority but God, who also gives his Holy Spirit to you."

Loving and following Jesus can also mean letting go of good relationships with the ones we love. "Whoever comes to me and does not hate father and mother, wife and children, brothers and sisters, yes, and even life itself, cannot be my disciple" (Luke 14:26). "Hating" our loved ones is used in the sense that we are willing to let go in order to do God's will. If we have to physically detach from them, as a cloistered monk or nun would do, we do so with great love, always remembering family and friends in our prayers. In other words, we detach without bitterness.

The opposite may be true in regard to relationships in which we experience negativity. Trying relationships that put Anonymous Monks to the test need not be severed immediately simply because they are difficult. Often, these relationships with difficult (sometimes impossible) people can teach us to rise to the highest contemplative gifts, one of which is the gift of clinging to God. [4]

Sometimes, when persons break free from difficult people, they are under the illusion that they have found peace because they are finally rid of the annoyance. This is the false peace of no longer having to love or deal with certain individuals.

The peace that comes from putting an end to enduring in love is a pseudo peace. It is not the peace of Christ. It is a peace that is "fraught with danger." [5] It is potentially deadly spiritually because we can be saying that we love God when all along we are only loving our own will. "Those who say, 'I love God,' and hate their brothers or sisters, are liars; for those who do not love a brother or sister whom they have seen, cannot love God whom they have not seen. The commandment we have from him is this: those who love God must love their brothers and sisters also" (1 John 4:20–21). As Anonymous Monks we experience union with God through properly ordered relationships with others.

1. *The Collected Works of St. John of the Cross*, p. 305.
2. *Catechism of the Catholic Church*, 1805.
3. *The Collected Works of St. John of the Cross*, p. 369.
4. Carthusian vocation literature: Charterhouse of the Transfiguration.
5. *John Cassian: Conferences*, 4, ch. VII.

⚂ Chapter 30 ⚃

Resolving Conflict Peacefully

If you have a dispute with someone,
make peace with him before the sun goes down.
RULE OF ST. BENEDICT, 4:73.

If an Anonymous Monk has a problem with someone, he or she tries first to sincerely pray for that person or persons. If after some time the same problem still exists and it is a serious matter, we need speak to that person or persons, personally expressing our perspective of the situation ever so meekly and ever so humbly. Remember Jesus' words, "If another member of the church sins against you, go and point out the fault when the two of you are alone. If the member listens to you, you have regained that one" (Matthew 18:15).

When expressing possibly confrontational opinions, Anonymous Monks prefer using words like "I feel," or "it seems to me as though," instead of making obstinate remarks such as "you always . . . ," or "you never. . . ." [1] If, after a humble exchange of perspectives takes place, there is still no real change, and if it is a serious matter, then we should seek outside help.

Following up on the above mentioned Scripture passage, Jesus continues, saying, "But if you are not listened to, take one or two others along with you, so that every word may be confirmed by the evidence of two or three witnesses" (Matthew 18:16). Preferably, then, we should seek the assistance of holy persons who can keep a confidence and who are willing to help resolve the issue by talking to all parties involved. If the person with whom we have an ongoing problem is a close family member, outside assistance may include medical doctors, counselors, and church clergy.

During this time of sharing and seeking advice from others, we must continue to be careful not to slander the other person or persons. We should try to explain conflicts in a calm, matter-of-fact manner, expressing a genuine love for all concerned. Anonymous Monks can remind themselves that the motivation for examining problematic issues is always the love of neighbor and the eternal good of all.

If there is still no resolution, we may need to seek the advice of other doctors, counselors, or clergy until the situation has been healed. All the while, we should take things slow and look at all conflicts as opportunities to advance in the higher, more unconditional levels of love. In this sense, an Anonymous Monk can truly thank God in all things, knowing that by trials of various sorts he or she is growing "mature and complete, lacking in nothing" (James 1:4).

If the same problem or problems still exist after many attempts at healing, and we are positively sure that we have done everything possible we know to do, we should continue to pray and believe that God will give us the grace to deal with the situation in a loving manner (2 Corinthians 12:9). "Offer right sacrifices, and put your trust in the LORD" (Psalm 4:5). I feel these days that many of us are too eager to ax various individuals out of our lives. We are living in an age where convenience is of much importance. This may be why the divorce rate in the United States is over 50 percent.

What I am about to say I say with much caution. If there is some reason so tragic that there appears to be no way of resolution then we can consider ever so cautiously and with much good counsel to apply the following text. If a person continues to sin, even though we have prayerfully taken all prudent steps to help him or her, as Jesus goes on to say in the same passage mentioned above, "If the offender refuses to listen even to the church, let such a one be to you as a Gentile and a tax collector" (Matthew 18:17).

Saint Benedict writes in his chapter entitled "Those Who Refuse to Amend After Frequent Reproofs": "Yet if even this procedure does not heal him, then finally, the abbot must use the knife and amputate. [Benedict sees the abbot as a skilled physician bringing health to his flock.] For the Apostle says, 'Banish the evil one from your midst'

(1 Corinthians 5:13); and again, 'If the unbeliever departs, let him depart' (1 Corinthians 7:15), lest one diseased sheep infect the whole flock." [2]

But again, it is with great reluctance that I have written the above because I have never had to take such drastic action with anyone in my forty-one years of life. I have heard of many persons eagerly cutting others out of their lives because of a lack of patience and in a spirit of bitterness. If you do take such drastic action be sure that your motivation is love. In the fear of the Lord, let us remember that whatever measure we use to judge others will be the same measure that God will use to judge us (Matthew 7:2).

1. *Rule of St. Benedict*, ch. 3:4.
2. *Rule of St. Benedict*, ch. 28:6–7.

🎐 Chapter 31 🎐

Maintaining
a Peaceful Routine

Are you hastening toward your heavenly home?
Then with Christ's help, keep this little rule
that we have written for beginners.
RULE OF ST. BENEDICT, 73:8.

For the Anonymous Monk, the search for peace and balance is a search for peace of mind and heart and, hopefully, the absence of anxiety. Any activity that may cause undue anxiety, such as public speaking, racing to get errands done, obsessing over completing household, work, and even church goals, should be kept in perspective. This is true even for the completion of the monastic practices mentioned in this book. Those who live with us or around us are often the best at letting us know when we are overdoing it. Most importantly, we hope to be in the present moment physically, mentally, and emotionally at all times.

Practicing the virtue of patience and fortitude, an Anonymous Monk hopes to resist the temptation of the so-called "rat race," racing toward the accomplishment of goals (even spiritual goals) instead of the contemplation of God.

When we are with our families and friends let us strive to give them 100 percent of our attention. Let us not be thinking about past failures, future goals, or possible problems. Instead, let's be as attentive to them as God is to us.

When we are on the telephone or having a face-to-face meeting with someone, let us try to give this person all of our attention by not speaking hurriedly and appearing as though we are rushing to end the conversation. If we feel that we cannot give people 100 percent of our attention, we can admit this to them. We would really like to speak with them but cannot give them our full attention at this time. We can ask them to visit or call at a better time. If we are rushing out the door or running out of time and the telephone rings, we may choose to think twice before picking it up, unless we are expecting an important call. In other words, we can avoid doing two things at once. Father Karunei Joseph, a wonderful priest, once said, "The present moment is the most sacred moment."

We can experience a beautiful deep union with others when we slow down and focus on the task at hand. As we listen we can be aware that our heart is open to hearing their ideas and their dreams, just as we would be open to God's ideas and dreams for our lives. By remaining open and purposefully uniting our will to the will of others, we experience a deep intimate love for others brought on by our loving submission. This does not mean that people are running all over us; it simply means that we seek to discern what is good about what they are saying and acknowledge that good.

Saint Benedict writes in his rule that if we have to turn someone away for a request, we should at least give this person a kind or encouraging word in return. [1] This is a good idea. It bonds us together so that even though we may have to reject another's ideas and requests, we have not rejected him or her as a person through an obstinate attitude. By opening our hearts to others we will experience a deep loving presence of God with all we meet and a peace that surpasses all understanding.

Being totally attentive to the present task is especially true in prayer. As Saint Benedict writes, "Let us stand to sing the Psalms in such a way that our minds are in harmony with our voices." [2] We cannot be in union with God and others unless we are in union within ourselves first.

The Anonymous Monk must focus his or her efforts on maintaining the balance between the Liturgy of the Hours (praying the Psalms), spiritual reading and study, and work. *"The Rule of St. Benedict*, basis of centuries of monastic observance, is often commended for its well-balanced structure. One element gives way to another in the course of the day, providing an alternating pattern that is both productive and refreshing."

1. *Rule of St. Benedict*, 31:6.
2. *Rule of St. Benedict*, 19:7.
3. "Statute on Unity and Pluralism," 1969, *Trappist Guidelines*, #3.

⚝ Chapter 32 ⚝
Gaining Strength
Through Adversity

Faithfully observing [Christ's] teachings [wherever
we happen to live] until death, we shall through patience
share in the sufferings of Christ that we may deserve
also to share in his kingdom.

RULE OF ST. BENEDICT, PROLOGUE: 50.

I n order for an Anonymous Monk to realize the grace of heroic virtue and courage, he or she must see it at work in the light of a heroic situation. It is often in the midst of extremely negative situations that a person can more clearly differentiate between the human and the divine. In other words, if we are wronged in a very serious, undeserved way, but yet can forgive, forget, and continue to love, that is heroic. The forgiving person is experiencing the heroic virtues of patience, forgiveness, and love.

In many seemingly tragic circumstances, a person is able to rise above and maintain a genuine loving attitude not only to serious offenders, but also to their own selves. This is heroic (divine) virtue. Many of us may have come to realize that it is simply not humanly possible to forgive certain things, but through the help of God's grace heroic (divine) virtue is possible.

The virtue of courage is often wrought through fighting the good fight of faith in the midst of many negative circumstances (2 Timothy 4:7). Like the heart of Mary being pierced seven times, courage stands unmoved in faith and becomes especially evident in the face of adversity (Luke 2:35), adversity such as contracting a disease, losing a job, suffering a broken relationship, going to prison, or feeling oppressed.

Negative circumstances pave the road to heroic courage, and courage is a virtue. I am saying that a person may not, nor does he or she need to, obtain courage without experiencing severely trying circumstances.

In times of persecution, instead of fleeing or hiding, Anonymous Monks should think of other persons who are in distress and do what they can to encourage them. This response includes simply praying, realizing that believers all over the world are undergoing the same or similar persecutions.

Many say that Judas Iscariot killed himself as a result of despair, primarily, the despair of believing that he could ever be forgiven for the part he played in the betrayal and ultimate crucifixion of Jesus (Matthew 26:47–50).

Could it be possible that Judas's despair was brought on by his refusal to love those who would undoubtedly loathe him for his betrayal of Jesus? Was his despair evidence to the fact that Judas really was not willing to undergo the same suffering, the same cup of salvation, the same death to which he, in effect, sentenced Jesus by his betrayal?

Did Judas have a premonition that there were those who would kill him for what he had done to Jesus? Had he, in essence, become like Haman? (Esther 7:10) Would he also be hung on the same gallows that he had constructed for Jesus? Had Judas become like King Saul who also committed suicide (1 Samuel 31:4) instead of facing the humility of admitting that repentance and doing good had the power to conquer evil? (Romans 12:21)

Could it be that Judas felt that the only way out, the only way of avoiding the humiliation of loving those who hated him, was to kill himself? Could it be that, rather than dying a death to self by humiliation (like Jesus), and loving those who hated him (like Jesus), Judas chose death to himself, murdering himself, suicide? Does not Judas exemplify those who would rather be dead than to sincerely love and forgive others, including themselves?

I feel compelled by God also to include as examples others who have refused to love, in particular the persons of Adolf Hitler and Joseph Paul Goebbels. Goebbels was a shrewd and cynical Nazi leader who not only helped usher millions of my Jewish loved ones to their death but also killed his wife, his beautiful children, and himself the day following Hitler's suicide. I hope that the innocent blood of the Goebbels' children bought mercy from God for him. [1]

"They served their idols, which became a snare to them. They sacrificed their sons and their daughters to the demons; they poured out innocent blood, the blood of their sons and daughters" (Psalm 106:36–38).

Could it be that they sentenced themselves to death and separation from God because they were unwilling to live the only way a person can live truly and experience true life, which is to love oneself and others, no matter what, simply because they exist? "God is love, and those who abide in love abide in God, and God abides in them" (1 John 4:16). Like Jesus, "No one has greater love than this, to lay down one's life for one's friends" (John 15:13).

1. *Encyclopedia International*, pp. 55–56.

⚑ Chapter 33 ⚑
Elevating Yourself Toward God

[We] must be chaste, temperate and merciful.
[We] should always "let mercy triumph over judgment"
(James 2:13) so that [we] too may win mercy.
RULE OF ST. BENEDICT, 64:9–10.

Elevation of the will toward God is when an Anonymous Monk is centered on loving God and doing God's will at every moment but is not thinking of anything in particular. The mind is more or less still and is resting. There are some things that might aid a person called to this type of prayer. Mainly, a person must be open to loving others as oneself. People whose minds are filled with resentment and bitterness will have difficulty with this type of prayer. It is also helpful not to be goal oriented in our thinking. This means that we can detach ourselves for a few moments from the many tasks that we must perform each day.

It will help us if we look at all activity as it truly is, as tasks to be performed for the love of God, whether we are changing a diaper, meeting the president, or writing a paperback novel. All are simply tasks. The lack of ego in our work will greatly aid us in our efforts to elevate our will to God. As an example, Thomas Aquinas, who could be considered as the Albert Einstein of theology, wrote many, many highly regarded writings. Toward the end of his life he had a vision in which it was revealed to him that everything he had ever written was so much "straw."

The point is that everything we can possibly do of any importance shrinks in the sight of God's eternal glory. The most important thing we could do is to look at others the way Mary looked at Jesus as a little child, her child. If we can see others the way their mothers saw them on the day they were born, then we will have a taste of the attitude of those in heaven. We must remember that God sees the entire person and remembers us from our conception in our mother's womb. This wonderful way of thinking aids us in the ability to free our minds and open our hearts to God.

Practically speaking, it can help clear our memories of clutter if we write lists of things that we need to remember to do. This is also why we need to be careful about what we watch and what we listen to before we pray. If we see something violent, or get in a fight with someone, this memory will be the first thing to crop up in our memories when we go to this type of prayer. These things are not worth losing the beauty of stilling our minds and our senses.

In this mode, the heart is wide open to the total will of God. Our hearts respond like Mary when she said, "Here am I, the servant of the Lord; let it be with me according to your word" (Luke 1:38). Like Mary, who did not consciously understand all the implications of being chosen to bear God's Son (Luke 1:34), neither do we use our power of understanding during the prayer known as "elevation of the will."

During the elevation of the will, we are locked in the perpetual "yes" of the Virgin Mary (Luke 1:38). We are not attempting to say or to think, only to "be," as in human "being." I am just "being." I am just existing in stillness. This is important because even the smartest person who ever lived had knowledge, which amounted to a pile of straw or a grain of sand on the seashores of the world compared to the knowledge that exists in God. We could also say that through the elevation of the will and stillness of the mind and senses we reach an awareness that there is knowledge far beyond what the human mind can comprehend.

This state is held up toward God like a burning torch of pure devotion. This was the "yes" of the Blessed Mother, a "yes" that rose above understanding to contemplate God in the darkness of faith. People who are totally comatose or "locked in" can even be seen to be in this state. This is the beauty of the state of the chronically ill—they are "locked in" a perpetual "yes" state. This torch of prayer is very powerful, and yet so many wish to extinguish it through euthanasia. Elevation of the will contains within it the power to save the whole world, just as Mary showed us at the Annunciation. It might be considered the gateway to salvation.

🔁 Chapter 34 🔁
Living Up to
the Grace of God

Trusting in God's help, [we] must in love obey.

RULE OF ST. BENEDICT, 68:5.

🔁O🔁ne of Saint William of St.-Thierry's most common themes was the idea that a person should do all that he can. [1] God often seems to meet people once they have done what they already know to do. Often in Scripture Jesus tells someone to "put out your hand" (Matthew 12:13) or "go wash" (John 9:7) before he heals them.

In other words, some action has to be performed in faith before God will intervene. As Anonymous Monks we seek to do all that we know to do before expecting anything extra from God.

When we have done all that we know to do, we experience the assurance that we have done all that we can. Having done all that we can, we experience a great sense of expectation. This expectation is often referred to in monastic writings as "keeping watch." "As the eyes of servants look to the hand of their master, as the eyes of a maid to the hand of her mistress, so our eyes are on the LORD our God, until he has mercy upon us" (Psalm 123:2). This state of expectancy is a powerful form of prayer whereby we become a "sentinel" (Psalm 130:6).

Our function is to guard Zion, the city of God (that is, the people of God). Oftentimes during the time of our watch, the Lord will impress upon us some divine knowledge for the advancement of the Kingdom, but this is usually only after we have done all that we already know to do. A monk may stay in this state of watching for hours before he is consciously aware of what God is saying. However, from the beginning of this "gazing," there is a sense of oneness with God. It is a oneness experienced by two lovers gazing at each other; words cannot adequately express the love that is exchanged between the two.

Even when we have done all we can do and are waiting for God's intervention, God intervenes freely and not on demand, not as a result of our acts, and not as if we have a strict right to it. We cannot coerce God's freedom by anything we do. That's why Jesus says, "When you have done all that is expected of you, say " 'we have done no more than our duty' " (Luke 17:10).

1. *The Golden Epistle*, p. 4.

ᕲ Chapter 35 ᕳ
Behold! All Things Are New!

Let them prefer nothing whatever to Christ,
and may he bring us all to everlasting life.

RULE OF ST. BENEDICT, 72:11–12.

By reading this book we have proven to ourselves and to God that we are now open to taking a new lease on life and converting to the point that we become a new creature. Let us make our new and renewed commitment to God more evident to ourselves by privately taking a religious name. Movie stars, radio announcers, and performers often take on new names to represent their new image. Why can't we as Christians also give ourselves a new name, following the example of God himself?

We see in Scripture that when a person is more deeply immersed in the work of God, God often changes their name. There are many references to this throughout Sacred Scripture. Saul's name was changed to Paul (Acts 13:9), Jacob's to Israel (Genesis 32:28), Abram's to Abraham (Genesis 17:5), and Sarai's to Sarah (Genesis 17:15).

Anonymous Monks should pick a name that represents someone from the communion of saints, someone who it seems has been directing them from beyond the grave. It might be the name of someone who had a similar path in life as ours. Someone that we can draw strength from, because they know in a special way what we have been going through. By taking on their name, in a sense, we continue their work together in a kindred spirit.

For instance, if we are wealthy we may consider taking on the name of Saint Katherine Drexel, who was very rich but yet became a saint.

If we are incarcerated, we might take the name of Saint Maximilian Kolbe, who was a prisoner in a concentration camp and then martyred. Of course, we may always pick the Blessed Mother Mary or Saint John the Baptist.

This secret religious name (close friends can know of it) will help us to accept and sacramentalize our special vocation. In other words, it will help to bring it out in the open, to make it more real. Taking on a religious name will help us to put on the "new self" and to avoid clinging to the past (Colossians 3:10). In times of temptation, unbelief, doubt, and fear, we can recall our religious name and give ourselves a reality check. Using our religious name as a source of strength and stability, we will remind ourselves of who and what we are in Christ.

In keeping with the Carthusian tradition of writing anonymously, Anonymous Monks must do all that they can, not to allow their name to be given any recognition, honor, or praise, remembering that we will receive our treasure in the next life. When an Anonymous Monk writes something spiritual for publication, he or she should seriously consider simply signing as "An Anonymous Monk."

If need be, we could also consider writing under a pen name, using our religious name, or writing in the name of another as did Pseudo-Dionysius, also known as Denys the Areopagite. Pseudo-Dionysius was a "pseudonymous writer of the fifth or sixth century" (*Encyclopedia of Catholicism*, p. 408.) Care must be taken, however, because there may be times when to write anonymously or using a pseudonym could be perceived as misleading, dishonest, or inappropriate. If this is the case, we can sign our names as an act of charity toward those who feel they need to know who we are for the sake of their own edification, be it spiritual or otherwise.

I have heard it said that Saint Anthony of Egypt, also known as the father of all monks, said something to the effect that "a monk reaches a point where he no longer knows who he is or what he is praying about." We can and will convert far beyond the person that is familiar to ourselves and to others. What a wonderful feeling to know that the old person literally passes away and all things mental, emotional, and physical about us and our relationships become healed and whole, fresh and new.

Conclusion

Day by day remind yourself that you are going to die.
RULE OF ST. BENEDICT, 4:47.

My love affair with Trappist monasticism began one evening when I felt compelled by the Holy Spirit to go to my local library to do some spiritual reading. As I perused the pages of the *Catholic Encyclopedia*, I saw the face of a man that struck me as the embodiment of everything that I ever wanted to become in Christ. In his face I saw many virtues at once: extreme sweetness, kindness, strength, love, manliness, courage, sensitivity, deep love, serenity, and understanding.

I had never seen Christ in anyone in my life who had even come close to the Christ-like beauty of this man in the picture. I guess you could say that in him I truly saw Christ incarnate. In his face I saw elements of everything that I ever hoped to become on my journey toward Christ. The fragments of good that were in me intertwined and I was healed by just one glance. It was immediately apparent that the man in the picture was endowed with special grace.

My first thought was that I wanted to be just like him. I had no idea who he was. Outwardly, as far as his clothing was concerned, he did not look religious at all. He was wearing the clothing and work gloves of a farmer. There was an earthiness about him that reminded me of my childhood and my love for the outdoors. It turned out to be a picture of Thomas Merton. I had never read any of his writings.

Since then, I have read many of his books and my love for Trappist monasticism has continued to grow. Trappist monasticism represents the arms that Christ has used to embrace me, the lips of Christ that give me life. This is why I love it so much and try to unite myself to my Trappist brothers and sisters by trying to live the monastic spirituality as best I can as an ordinary person, as an Anonymous Monk.

Outwardly, I may appear to have many possessions—car, house, and more. I actually hope this situation changes. Today, I asked the Lord to make me poor. I wish to experience a poverty that I once was told existed among some severely oppressed prisoners in a penal settlement located in French Guiana called Devil's Island. As in the Jewish Holocaust, these men were confined to cages and cells. Many were placed in solitary confinement and shut up in total darkness for months on end. I heard of one man who lived in darkness and solitary confinement for over fifteen years. This interior sense of solitude is what I wish to experience. May God provide for me to fulfill so high a calling someday.

As for now, I hope to join the poor. I will try to joyfully give all that I possess to those who persecute me. After all, if the prisoners on Devil's Island and the Jews slaughtered in the Holocaust could endure such great persecution and suffering, how much more could and should every Christian, even those of least renown, gladly give up all for the cause of one so great as Jesus, the Son of Man and the Son of God.

Part of me cannot live for the things of this world and be happy, knowing that my brothers and sisters are living chronically ill, oppressed, unloved, and imprisoned. I will strive to unite myself to the poorest of the poor. I hope to stay by their sides by uniting myself to them at least in spirit. With the help of God's grace, I hope to seek nothing as they have nothing, and to live for God alone.

I am concerned that I cannot be in a heaven where I know that some of my other selves may have been excluded. Like Saint Paul, I could gladly live in hell for eternity if it meant that my other selves could enter eternal bliss because of my presence there (Romans 9:3). Some may think that what I am describing is an interior hell, a hell of seclusion, poverty, oppression, a place of sacrifice. But to me, being an Anonymous Monk is true living.

Saint Benedict writes that by our perseverance in humility we will learn something about perfect love. That which we once performed with dread, we will now begin to observe without effort, as though naturally from habit, no longer out of fear of hell, but out of love for Christ, good habit and delight in virtue. [1] We will come to realize that our austerities have led us only to the beginning. We will have arrived to the point of realizing just how slothful we actually were and that now as Anonymous Monks our hearts are finally truly set on the journey. [2]

I have great joy in knowing and believing, without doubt, that our living as Anonymous Monks is the cause of many person's passing over to Christ, the beloved Son of God. And what is this joy that we have but the joy of one who has been chosen to die for one's children that they might live. It is the joy of Christ and of the Father and of the Holy Spirit, who died for their children!

What good parent would not run to their own death, bursting with joy, if it meant that their terminally ill child would live. This is the joy of God and of his angels in heaven. And do you know why there is joy in heaven? Because God died and saved his children who were dead and dying, the dream fulfilled of every good parent. These children are our gift to the one we love. They are our union with him.

We stand before God as Anonymous Monks as a constant reminder that his Son died for our other selves. In a way, like the children of a man and woman who are married, these are our children, the souls that benefit from our union and death in him. I am ready to be open and honest about these desires that God has placed within my soul. My prayer for you is that you, and many others to follow, will grow ever deeper in that love which is Christ. With the help of God's grace, I pray that you continue to "stand on your own feet." Amen.

1. *Rule of St. Benedict*, 7:68, 69.
2. *Rule of St. Benedict*, 73:7.

🖋 Appendix I 🖋

How to Pray . . .

The Psalms

We may pray the Psalms, as explained below, as often as we are able.
Some may wish to pray as often as seven times a day. (Psalm 119:164
actually reads, "Seven times a day I praise you. . . .) However,
everyone's schedule varies, so each should pray as he or she can. If you
do pray seven times a day, saying three Psalms each time, you will find
that you will have prayed 147 of the 150 Psalms in a week's time. We
should add an extra Psalm to three of our prayer times on the seventh
day if we wish to complete the Psalms each week.

To pray the Psalms, begin by making the sign of the cross and saying
these words:

> Oh God, come to my assistance.
> Oh Lord, make haste to help me.
> Glory be to the Father,
> and to the Son,
> and to the Holy Spirit,
> as it was in the beginning,
> is now, and ever shall be,
> world without end.
> Amen.

Then sing a hymn. It could be as simple as "Jesus loves me."
Or you might want to make up your own.

Then say three entire Psalms, for example:

Psalm 1, verses 1–6,
Psalm 2, verse 1–12,
and Psalm 3, verses 1–8.

At the end of each Psalm say:

Glory to the Father,
and to the Son,
and to the Holy Spirit,
as it was in the beginning,
is now, and ever shall be,
world without end.
Amen.

After you have recited the Psalms, read a few lines of Scripture or other sacred writings if you have them.

Then say the Our Father:

Our Father, Who are in heaven,
holy is your name,
your kingdom come,
your will be done,
on earth as it is in heaven.
Give us this day our daily bread,
and forgive us our trespasses
as we forgive those who trespass against us.
And lead us not into temptation,
but deliver us from evil.
For the kingdom, the power, and the glory are yours,
now and forever. Amen.

Then say the Hail, Holy Queen:

Hail, Holy Queen,
Mother of Mercy,
our life, our sweetness and our hope,

to you do we cry poor banished children of Eve,
to you do we send up our sighs,
mourning and weeping in this valley of tears.
Turn then, most gracious advocate,
your eyes of mercy toward us,
and after this our exile,
show unto us the blessed fruit of your womb, Jesus.
O clement, O loving, O sweet Virgin Mary,
Pray for us, O Holy Mother of God,
that we may be worthy of the promises of Christ.

Then close by saying:

May the divine assistance remain always with us,
and with our brothers and sisters who have passed away.
And may the souls of all the faithfully departed,
through the mercy of God, rest in peace.
Amen.

Let us bless the Lord.
Thanks be to God.

The Angelus

(Usually recited at 6:00 A.M., noon, and after evening prayer.)

The angel of the Lord declared unto Mary.
And she conceived by the Holy Ghost.

Hail, Mary, full of grace, the Lord is with you.
Blessed are you among women
and blessed is the fruit of your womb, Jesus.

Holy Mary, Mother of God,
pray for us sinners,
now, and at the hour of our death.
Amen.

And the word became flesh and dwelt among us.

Hail, Mary, full of grace, the Lord is with you.
Blessed are you among women
and blessed is the fruit of your womb, Jesus.

Holy Mary, Mother of God,
pray for us sinners,
now, and at the hour of our death.
Amen.

Pray for us, O holy Mother of God.
That we may be made worthy of the promises of Christ.

Let us pray.

Pour forth, we beseech Thee, O Lord,
thy grace into our hearts,
that we to whom the incarnation of Christ, Thy Son,
was made known by the message of an angel,
may by his passion and cross,
be brought to the glory of his resurrection
through the same Christ our Lord.
Amen.

The Rosary

When praying the Rosary, we reflect on various aspects of the life of Christ until they actually become a part of us. There are three basic parts of the life of Christ that we think about as we pray. They are the joyful times, the sorrowful times, and the glorious times. Most people do not realize that the Rosary is a meditation. We recite this prayer as we think about the different times of Jesus' life. If we decide to pray the joyful times, we think about each joyful event listed below as we pray.

For example: when the angel came to Mary and told her that she was going to have a son, we say one Our Father and then ten Hail Marys, and finish with a Glory Be to the Father. As we ponder, we may relate this to ourselves as Jesus coming to us and telling us that he wants to be born again in us. So, as we pray, we try to relate the events of Jesus' life to ourselves personally.

Then we reflect on the second joyful time, which is the visitation and repeat the same pattern of prayers, one Our Father, ten Hail Marys, and one Glory Be to the Father, as we ponder the mystery. The important thing is that we ponder as we pray. Just praying the best you can and for as long as you are able brings peace. If you have to stop, then be grateful for the time the Lord has given.

When praying the Rosary, we begin with the sign of the cross:

In the name of the Father and the Son and the Holy Spirit. Amen.

Then we say the Apostles' Creed:

I believe in God the Father Almighty,
Creator of heaven and earth:
and in Jesus Christ, his only Son, our Lord:
who was conceived by the Holy Spirit,
born of the Virgin Mary;
suffered under Pontius Pilate,
was crucified, died and was buried.
He descended into hell,
the third day he rose again from the dead;
he ascended into heaven,
sits at the right hand of God the Father Almighty;
from thence he shall come to judge
the living and the dead.
I believe in the Holy Spirit,
the Holy Catholic Church,
the communion of saints,
the forgiveness of sins,
the resurrection of the body,
and the life of the world to come.
Amen.

Then we say one Our Father:

Our Father, who are in heaven,
holy is your name,
your kingdom come,
your will be done,
on earth as it is in heaven.
Give us this day our daily bread,
and forgive us our trespasses
as we forgive those
who trespass against us.
And lead us not into temptation,
but deliver us from evil.
For the kingdom, the power, and the glory
are yours, now and forever.
Amen.

Then we say three Hail Marys:

Hail, Mary, full of grace,
the Lord is with you.
Blessed are you among women
and blessed is the fruit of your womb, Jesus.

Holy Mary, Mother of God,
pray for us sinners,
now, and at the hour of our death.
Amen.

Following the Hail Mary, we pray one Glory Be to the Father:

Glory to the Father
and to the Son,
and to the Holy Spirit,
As it was in the beginning,
is now, and ever shall be,
world without end.
Amen.

After praying these introductory prayers, we pray one Our Father, ten Hail Marys, and a Glory Be to the Father for each of the five following joyful mysteries:

The Joyful Mysteries

1. The Annunciation
We think of God wanting to be born in us, as when the angel came to Mary and told her that she would have a son.

2. The Visitation
We think of helping others in need, like Mary who went to visit her cousin Elizabeth and help her when she was pregnant with John the Baptist.

3. The Nativity
We think about not living in luxury and being humble like Jesus who was born in a stable.

4. The Presentation
We think about how Jesus truly is the one who saves us, as was mentioned in Scripture when Jesus was a baby being presented to God in the temple.

5. Finding Jesus in the Temple
We think about how desperately we should look for Jesus, as did Mary and Jesus when they lost Jesus and found him with the spiritual leaders in the temple.

After praying the one Our Father, ten Hail Marys, and a Glory Be to the Father for each joyful event of Jesus' life, we conclude by reciting the following prayer to Mary called the Hail, Holy Queen:

Hail, Holy Queen,
Mother of Mercy,
our life, our sweetness and our hope,
to you do we cry poor banished children of Eve,

to you do we send up our sighs,
mourning and weeping in this valley of tears.
Turn then, most gracious advocate,
your eyes of mercy toward us,
and after this our exile,
show unto us the blessed fruit of your womb, Jesus.
O clement, O loving, O sweet Virgin Mary,
Pray for us, O Holy Mother of God,
that we may be worthy of the promises of Christ.

Let us pray.

O God, whose only begotten Son,
by his life, death, and resurrection,
has purchased for us the rewards of eternal life,
grant, we beseech thee,
that by meditating on these mysteries
of the most holy Rosary
of the Blessed Virgin Mary,
we may imitate what they contain,
and obtain what they promise,
through the same Christ our Lord.
Amen.

May the divine assistance remain always with us,
and with our brothers and sisters who have passed away.
And may the souls of all the faithfully departed,
through the mercy of God, rest in peace.
Amen.

In the name of the Father,
and of the Son,
and of the Holy Spirit.
Amen.

If we wish to continue and think about the sorrowful times or the glorious times of Jesus' life, they are listed below.

The Sorrowful Mysteries

1. The Agony in the Garden
We think about Jesus in the garden surrendering himself to death.

2. The Scourging at the Pillar
We think about Jesus being beaten.

3. The Crowning with Thorns
We think about Jesus being mocked.

4. Jesus Carrying His Cross
We think of the weight of the cross and Jesus' suffering.

5. The Crucifixion
We think about Jesus loving us so much that he was willing to die a horrible death.

Again, after praying one Our Father, ten Hail Marys, and a Glory Be to the Father for each sorrowful event of Jesus' life, we conclude by reciting the Hail, Holy Queen, as provided above.

If we wish to continue reflecting on the glorious times of Jesus' life, they are listed below.

The Glorious Mysteries

1. Jesus' Resurrection
We think of Jesus' victory over death.

2. The Ascension
We think of Jesus now in heaven preparing a place for us.

3. The Descent of the Holy Spirit
We think that now we have the Holy Spirit here with us to give us strength.

4. The Assumption
We think of Mary being lifted to heaven, body and soul.

5. The Coronation of Mary

We think that we will also be crowned as was Mary if we remain faithful.

And again after praying one Our Father, ten Hail Marys, and a Glory Be to the Father for each joyful event of Jesus' life, we conclude by reciting the Hail, Holy Queen, as provided above.

✎ Appendix II ✎

Vocation Information

For General Religious
Vocation Information,
Contact:

Vocations Placement Service, Inc.
6311 NW 47 Court
Coral Springs, FL 33067
954-340-5705
Vocationsplacement.org

For Trappist Monastery Information,
Contact:

International Internet
Directory for Men:
http://www.rc.net/ocso/drcty_m.htm

Locations for Men within
the United States:

Abbey of Gethsemani
3642 Monks Road
Trappist, KY 40051
(502) 549-3117

Abbey of the Holy Trinity
1250 South 9500 East
Huntsville, UT 84317
(801) 745-3784

Holy Cross Abbey
901 Cool Spring Lane
Berryville, VA 22611-2700
(540) 955-1425

Mepkin Abbey
1098 Mepkin Abbey Road
Moncks Corner, SC 29461
(843) 761-8509

Monastery of the Holy Spirit
2625 Highway 212, SW
Conyers, GA 30208
(770) 483-8705

New Melleray Abbey
6500 Melleray Circle
Peosta, IA 52068
(319) 588-2319

Our Lady of Guadalupe Abbey
P.O. Box 97
Lafayette, OR 97127
(503) 852-7174

Our Lady of New Clairvaux
P.O. Box 80
Vina, CA 96092
(530) 839-2161

Our Lady of the Genessee Abbey
P.O. Box 900
Piffard, NY 14533
(716) 243-0660

St. Benedict's Abbey
1012 Monastery Road
Snowmass, CO 81654
(970) 927-3311

St. Joseph's Abbey
167 N. Spencer Road
Spencer, MA 01562
(508) 885-8700

International Internet
Directory for Women:
http://www.rc.net/ocso/drcty_f.htm

Locations for Women
within the United States:

Mount St. Mary's Abbey
300 Arnold Street
Wrentham, MA 02093
(508) 528-1282

Our Lady of the Angels
3365 Monastery Drive
Crozet, VA 22932
(804) 823-1452

Our Lady of the Mississippi Abbey
8400 Abbey Hill
Dubuque, IA 52003
(319) 582-2595

Redwoods Monastery
Whitethorn, CA 95589
(707) 986-7419

Santa Rita Abbey
HC 1
P.O. Box 929
Sonoita, AZ 85637
(520) 455-5595

☙ Appendix III ❧

Bibliography

"Dogmatic Constitution on the Church" (Lumen gentium), ch. 5, "The Call to Holiness." *The Documents of Vatican II*, Walter M. Abbott, S.J., ed. New York, NY: America Press, 1966.

John Cassian: Conferences, Classics of Western Spirituality. Dr. Colm Luibheid, translator and editor. Mahwah, NJ: Paulist Press, 1985.

Christian Prayer, Catholic Book Publishing Co., Totowa, NJ, 1976.

Carthusian Spirituality: The Writings of Hugh of Balma and Guigo de Ponte, Classics of Western Spirituality. Hugh of Balma, ed. New York, NY: Paulist Press, 1997.

Climacus, John, *The Ladder of Divine Ascent*, Brookline, MA: Holy Transfiguration Monastery, 1997.

Diemer, Paul, O.C.S.O. *Love Without Measure*, Kalamazoo, MI: Cistercian Publications, 1990.

Encyclopedia of Catholicism. Richard P. McBrien, general editor. New York, NY: HarperCollins Publishers, 1995.

"General Chapter of the Cistercian Order of the Strict Observance," *Statutes on Unity and Pluralism (The Constitution & Statues of the Nuns of the Cistercian Order of the Strict Observance)*. US: 1990.

Hermann, Dorothy, *Helen Keller: A Life*, Chicago, IL: University of Chicago Press, 1999.

John of the Cross, "Ascent of Mount Carmel." Kieran Kavanaugh, ed. *Collected Works of St. John of the Cross*, Washington, DC: ICS Publications, 1979.

Merriam-Webster Dictionary, Springfield, MA: Merriam Webster, Inc., 1995.

Merton: A Film Biography. Produced by Paul Wilkes and Audrey Glynn. New York, NY: First Run/Icarus Films. 1984.

Merton, Thomas. *Disputed Questions*, San Diego, CA: Harcourt Brace and Company, 1985.

———. *The Inner Experience*, Cistercian Studies. Huntsville, UT: Holy Trinity Abbey, copyright 1983 by the Trustees of the Merton Legacy Trust.

———. *The Intimate Merton: His Life from His Journals.* Patrick Hart and Jonathan Montaldo, editors. New York, NY: HarperCollins, 1999.

———. *Love and Living,* San Diego, CA: Harcourt Brace and Company, 1985.

———. *Marxism and Monastic Perspectives.* Naomi Burton, Brother Patrick Hart, James Laughlin, editors; Amiya Chakravarty, consulting editor. New York, NY: New Directions, 1975.

———. *Thoughts in Solitude,* New York, NY: Farrar Straus & Giroux, 1958.

Microsoft Encarta 98 Encyclopedia, 1998, 1993-1997 Microsoft Corporation. All rights reserved.

"Nicene Creed," *Encyclopedia of Catholicism.* Richard P. McBrien, general editor. New York, NY: HarperCollins Publishers, 1995, p. 917.

"*Nuns in the Charterhouse of Notre Dame.*" Carthusian Vocational Literature. Charterhouse of the Transfiguration, Chartreuse Notre-Dame: France.

Palmer, G.E., *The Philokalia: The Complete Text,* Winchester, MA: Faber and Faber, Inc. 1985.

Pope John Paul II, *Catechism of the Catholic Church,* Des Plaines, IL: Double Day, 1995.

The Rule of St. Benedict in English, Timothy Fry, O.S.B., ed. Collegeville, MN: The Liturgical Press, 1982.

Tertullian, "The Apparel of Women," Edwin A. Quain, S.J., translator. *The Fathers of the Church,* Volume 40, New York, NY: Fathers of the Church, Inc., 1959.

Ward, Sr. Benedicta, *Sayings of the Desert Fathers,* Kalamazoo, MI: Cistercian Studies, 1987.

William of St. Thierry, *The Golden Epistle: A Letter to the Brethren at Mont Dieu,* Kalamazoo, MI: Cistercian Publications, 1980.

Zanzig Thomas, *Understanding Catholic Christianity,* Winona, MI: St. Mary's Press, 1997, p. 1.